OSPREY COMBAT AIRCRAFT 108

A-3 SKYWARRIOR UNITS OF THE VIETNAM WAR

SERIES EDITOR TONY HOLMES

OSPREY COMBAT AIRCRAFT 108

A-3 SKYWARRIOR UNITS OF THE VIETNAM WAR

RICK MORGAN

OSPREY
PUBLISHING

Front Cover

Naval Aviation is a brotherhood, where men will do heroic things in impossible conditions for each other even when your aircraft is a large, highly vulnerable, twin-engined bomber full of fuel without the luxury of ejection seats for the crew of three.

On the morning of 18 July 1967 the carrier USS *Oriskany* (CVA-34) was sending strike aircraft from Carrier Air Wing 16 deep 'over the beach' to hit bridges located near Phu Ly, in North Vietnam. Things went bad from the start as the A-4E of VA-164's Lt Cdr Richard Hartman was hit by 37 mm AAA near the target. He ejected, and his wingman, Lt(jg) Larry Duthie, immediately started to cover his lead for potential rescue. Duthie, in another Skyhawk from VA-164, was then hit by AAA as well and he tried to head towards the water. Duthie made it about 12 miles east before he too had to eject. With two men on the ground deep in enemy territory all other missions immediately became Search and Rescue (SAR). Among the first to arrive on the scene was Lt Cdr Dick Schaffert, flying an F-8C Crusader from VF-111.

Schaffert set up a SARCAP over Duthie while dodging anti-aircraft fire and the odd SA-2 Surface-to-Air Missile (SAM). After 45 minutes in the area he finally turned over the on-scene commander duties and headed back to the Gulf of Tonkin, even though his efforts had left him without sufficient fuel to reach the North Vietnamese coast, let alone CVA-34.

Safely orbiting well over the Gulf of Tonkin, Lt Cdr Tom Maxwell of VAH-4 Detachment Golf was piloting the duty KA-3B Skywarrior tanker whilst monitoring the SAR event on the radio. When Schaffert's call for help came he looked at his two crewmates, Lt(jg) Jim Vanderhoek and ADJ1 Bill Shelton, who immediately gave him an emphatic 'Thumbs Up'. Then, against standing orders, he turned the 'Whale' westward and flew it inland to find the fuel-starved fighter. A consummate tanker pilot in extreme circumstances, Maxwell saw the F-8, timed the rendezvous perfectly and wheeled his Skywarrior in front of the thirsty Crusader while Vanderhoek extended the refuelling hose. Schaffert, with his fuel needle bouncing off zero, connected on his first plug and was relieved to see it moving up as they headed for the coast – all this while flak burst

nearby and their radar warning gear alerted them to SAM activity in the vicinity.

Both aircraft were able to recover back onboard *Oriskany* because of the courage and skill of the 'Whale' crew. Duthie was rescued by a USAF HH-3E Jolly Green Giant helicopter the following day, but not before the loss of another A-4E, the pilot of which was able to reach the Gulf of Tonkin prior to ejecting. Attempts to reach Hartman, however, led to the loss of a US Navy H-3 Sea King and its crew of four. Hartman became a PoW and subsequently died in captivity.

Because they had violated Seventh Fleet orders and taken their aircraft over North Vietnam, Maxwell and his crew would not be rewarded with any personal decorations for their actions. The KA-3B involved would be destroyed three months later after a failed JATO launch from Cubi Point, in the Philippines (*Cover artwork by Gareth Hector*)

First published in Great Britain in 2015 by Osprey Publishing
PO Box 883, Oxford, OX1 9PL, UK
PO Box 3985, New York, NY 10185-3985, USA

E-mail: info@ospreypublishing.com

Osprey Publishing is part of the Osprey Group

© 2015 Osprey Publishing Limited

A CIP catalogue record for this book is available from the British Library

ISBN: 978 1 4728 0564 5
PDF e-book ISBN: 978 1 4728 0565 2
e-Pub ISBN: 978 1 4728 0566 9

Edited by Tony Holmes
Cover Artwork by Gareth Hector (www.garethhector.co.uk/aviation-art/)
Aircraft Profiles by Jim Laurier
Index by Fionbar Lyons
Originated by PDQ Digital Media Solutions, UK
Printed in China through Worldprint Ltd

16 17 18 19   10 9 8 7 6 5 4 3 2

Osprey Publishing is supporting the Woodland Trust, the UK's leading woodland conservation charity, by funding the dedication of trees.

www.ospreypublishing.com

Acknowledgements

I need to thank the following people who helped in the development of this book; Rear Admiral Lyle Bull US Navy (Ret), Lt Cdr Rick Burgess US Navy (Ret), Cdr Pete Clayton US Navy (Ret), Lt Cdr Dick Damron US Navy (Ret), Capt Rich Dann US Naval Reserve, Capt Curt Dose US Navy (Ret), Capt Larry Kaiser US Navy (Ret), PHCS Bob Lawson US Navy (Ret), Capt Tom Maxwell US Navy (Ret), Cdr Peter Mersky US Naval Reserve (Ret), Lt Cdr Dave Ouellette US Navy (Ret), Capt Dick Schaffert US Navy (Ret), Cdr Doug Siegfried US Navy (Ret), Capt Dick Toft US Navy (Ret), Capt T J Williams US Navy (Ret), Tony Holmes, Angelo Romano, Tommy Thomason and Frank McBaine. Finally, many thanks to the A-3 Skywarrior Association for its help – www.a3skywarrior.com

CONTENTS

AUTHOR'S INTRODUCTION

My personal association with the A-3 was short – only about two years, and my squadronmates would tell you not very notable, but during that time with VAQ-33 in Key West I developed a strong affinity for both the Douglas Skywarrior and those who flew it. When ordered into A-3s from VT-25 in 1980 I asked my XO, Cdr Bob Kiem (an A-7 pilot) what he thought of the aircraft, and he told me 'It's a real Cadillac. You're going to love it'. Many who flew the mighty 'Whale' would certainly agree with his assessment, as it was truly an aircraft of myth and legend.

Among its many traits, perhaps longevity and utility best describe the type, as there is no doubt that the A-3 was a remarkably long-lived aircraft that excelled at every job it was given. While never gaining the spotlight or ink of, say, the F-4 Phantom II, A-4 Skyhawk or F-14 Tomcat, it was arguably deserving of recognition as 'Best Supporting Actor' for its value to Naval Aviation. I have included several stories representing the A-3's criticality to the air wing from the perspective of other Naval Aviators to highlight this point.

Of course it is truly fortunate that the type never had to carry out its initial role – nuclear strike – but the basic adaptability of the airframe led to the A-3's use for 35 years, from 1956 through to 1991, as a bomber, tanker, VIP transport, electronic warfare (EW) aircraft, photo-reconnaissance platform, high-speed COD, trainer and developmental airframe. Once done with the US Navy the Skywarrior would continue to fly as a contractor testbed. This lifespan even surprised a good number of its most ardent supporters, as the US Navy seemed to run an 'annual A-3 retirement drill' after Vietnam. The fact was that the Skywarrior was just too important to give up. While its USAF half-cousin, the B-66 Destroyer, vanished within two years of war's end, the A-3 still had more than 30 years left in it.

The 'Whale', as it was universally known, garnered respect, and usually awe, from practically everyone who knew it. The aeroplane's size was always a source of amazement for those on the flightdeck, no matter what carrier it was working from. The type's longevity is demonstrated by the observation that when the first A3Ds deployed in USS *Forrestal* (CVA-59) in January 1957 with VAH-1 they shared the deck with F9F-8 Cougars, FJ-3M Furies and F2H Banshees. By the late 1980s VQ-1 and VQ-2 EA-3Bs were rubbing shoulders with F-14 Tomcats, F/A-18 Hornets and EA-6B Prowlers. No other jet aircraft flown by the US Navy enjoyed such longevity.

Rarely acknowledged by Naval Aviators and historians alike, the 'Whale' served with six different types of squadron – VAH, VAQ, VQ, VAP/VCP, VR and VAK. It was, unarguably, a timeless and classic carrier aircraft that spanned the generations. Perhaps the most remarkable thing about the A-3 is that its celebrated chief engineer, Ed Heinemann, was told in the late 1940s that the aeroplane he said could be built was impossible. Heinemann, of course, proved the naysayers wrong.

Over the years the multitude of A-3 variants have confounded many, which has led to a good deal of misinformation appearing on the type in print. Throughout the book I use the terms 'bomber' and 'version' to denote the two primary A-3 designs. The 'bombers' were the A3D-1 (A-3A) and A3D-2 (A-3B), which were all bomb-bay equipped aircraft, and their derivatives include the KA-3B and EKA-3B. The 'versions' are the three special mission types with equipment and/or men in the fuselage, and they include the EA-3B, RA-3B and TA-3B.

The differences between the sub-variants have led to a lot of confusion over the years among writers and historians. While there was certainly an A3D, which became the A-3 in the Department of Defense re-designation drill of 1962, there was never an 'A-3D', as is all-too-frequently written, let alone things like an 'EA-3D', 'KA-3D' or even as one misguided author put it an 'EA3-2Q'. Likewise, the electronic reconnaissance EA-3B (A3D-2Q) and EKA-3B jammer/tanker are completely different 'Whales' with distinct mission sets that are also frequently confused.

This effort is not presented as a definitive work on the A-3 series, nor can it be in the space provided. I wrote this book with the aim of trying to cover three specific areas – the technical details of the airframe, its fleet operations and the men who flew it, with a focus on the decade from 1964 to 1974.

Although the bulk of this work covers the period in Vietnam, I've also included chapters on the years before and after as bookends of sorts in order to help tell the greater story and provide context for the rest. Keeping with the book's primary time frame, the colour profiles all come from Vietnam-related deployments or squadrons. Picking 30 specific airframes proved more difficult than I had originally thought it would be as the number of Skywarrior cruises during Vietnam led to some very colourful aircraft and unique markings. I think you will agree that artist Jim Laurier has done a magnificent job of depicting them. Likewise, Gareth Hector's cover art is among the best he has ever done.

The photographs in this work have come from a number of great sources, including the US Navy itself, the Tailhook Association, Peter Mersky and Angelo Romano in particular. Several of the men interviewed were also able to help, especially Tom Maxwell and Dave Ouellette. Requests for photographs led to numerous side-stories, including one somewhat embittered former 'Whale' pilot who told me he had sold everything he had relating to his time as a Naval Aviator because he could not stand to look at his US Navy possessions anymore. Another vet told me, in a wonderful southern drawl, 'Well, Rick, I'd love to help, but my first wife got those pictures in the settlement and I'm pretty sure she burned them all'.

For those looking for information on the 'Whale's' USAF half-cousin, the Douglas B-66 Destroyer, you will have to find another source. Although frequently referred to simply as 'the Air Force's A-3', it was never that simple, as although it may have started that way, the B-66 ended up a very different design with completely different powerplants (Allison J71s), auxiliaries, wing form, radar/bomb systems and, perhaps most significantly, ejection seats for its crew. When comparing the two types, one US Navy aircrewman that had time in both put it best when he stated that 'the only thing the two aircraft shared was the shadow on the ramp'. To do it proper justice, the Destroyer deserves a separate book to cover its heroic work in Vietnam.

The author has nothing but respect for those who flew the 'Whale' off the boat. They remain a very unique group of Naval Aviators, Naval Flight Officers and Aircrew who flew this magnificent aircraft in challenging conditions. It is to those men that this book is dedicated.

ORIGINS OF HEAVY ATTACK

The need for what became 'Heavy Attack' was quickly established after World War 2 as the US Navy came to the conclusion that to remain viable in the post-war period it had to develop its own atomic strike capability. The US Navy remembered the impact the Halsey-Doolittle Raid on Tokyo had had in April 1942, and it worked throughout the rest of World War 2 trying to develop a realistic twin-engined, carrier-based bomber concept for use after the war. The introduction of atomic weapons in 1945 further emphasised the direction the service felt it needed to go.

The huge new *Midway* class aircraft carriers that had come on line at the end of the war offered the opportunity for the US Navy to deploy a sea-based deep-strike capability like the world had never seen. This, of course, quickly turned into a 'turf war' with the new US Air Force as both services fought over who would dominate post-war defence budgets. Not surprisingly, the junior service advocated long-range atomic strike from land bases, largely in the form of the huge, new B-36 Peacemaker strategic bomber. Its supporters believed that this capability rendered conventional forces, and US Navy aircraft carriers in particular, obsolete. This in turn led to the 'Revolt of the Admirals' where senior US Navy officers overtly and covertly lobbied for more carriers to ensure, in their view, the very future of Naval Aviation. They felt that the latter was under imminent threat following the cancellation of the new carrier USS *United States* (CVB-58) in 1948 by President Harry S Truman's administration.

However, the start of the Korean War in 1950 quickly reminded the world of the continued strategic utility and military requirement of aircraft carriers and their embarked carrier air groups. The US Navy went from only seven fleet carriers (three CVBs and four CVs) in service at the start of the war to 14 (now all designated CVAs) by July 1953. More important was the renewed development of what would soon be called a 'supercarrier', the vessel in question being commissioned at Newport News shipyard, in Virginia, in 1955 in the form of the remarkable 60,000 ton USS *Forrestal* (CVA-59), named after the nation's first Secretary of Defense.

Initial attempts to operate atomic-capable strike aircraft at sea centred on the interim use of Lockheed P2V Neptunes in a carrier environment. The normally land-based patrol aeroplane had to be craned onboard in a suitable port and then launched using Jet Assisted Take-Off (JATO) bottles. Unable to recover back onboard the ship, the P2V landed on the beach. The first such launch was in April 1948 and, although impressive, combat would have almost certainly involved a one-way mission for the

Laying the groundwork for the US Navy's Heavy Attack community was the North American AJ Savage. Largely unloved, the ungainly AJ set the carrier navy up for the A3D Skywarrior. This is an AJ-2 from VAH-6, operating on USS *Lexington* (CVA-16) in 1956. Heavy Six would move to Whidbey in 1958 for A3D transition and then transfer to Sanford and re-equip with Vigilantes before the start of the Vietnam War (*Rich Dann Collection*)

crew. Use of the P2V was restricted to *Midway* class decks, and although widely heralded, it was only a temporary solution that had to be followed by a truly carrier-capable aircraft. The next step soon came in the form of the North American AJ Savage.

The Savage was a huge carrier aircraft for its time, with a pair of piston engines and a jet buried in the fuselage to increase maximum speed. First flown in May 1949, the AJ carried a crew of three. Its maximum launch weight was 54,000 lbs (more than twice that of the next-heaviest aircraft in the carrier air group at the time, the AD-4 Skyraider) and 37,500 lbs for arrested landing. Its combat radius, with weapon, was about 700 nautical miles.

Organisationally, the US Navy chose to use the Composite (VC) designation for the squadrons that would take the Savage to sea. During World War 2 'Comprons' typically flew both TBF Avengers and F4F/FM Wildcats off escort (CVE) carriers in anti-submarine and fleet support roles. After the conflict the service established almost 20 new VC units to supply detachments to carriers in specialist mission areas. By the end of the decade these squadrons had formed the basis for a number of carrier-deployed communities, including Heavy Attack (VAH), Nightfighter and Attack (VFAW and VAAW), Light Photo-Reconnaissance (VFP), Airborne Early Warning (VAW) and Anti-Submarine (VS).

When deployed, the AJ was able to work off both *Midway* and modified-*Essex* class ships, although the type quickly gained a reputation for being both temperamental and challenging to operate in a carrier environment. Carrier personnel used to dealing with small tactical aircraft frequently had issues with the AJ. The aircraft's hydraulic system tended to leak and its other quirks quickly led it to become the bane of flightdeck crews throughout the US Navy. For many boat COs the AJs remained a 'pain in the arse', and they were frequently off-loaded into places like Atsugi, Japan, or Port Lyautey, Morocco, where they would stand ground alert and be ready to return to the carrier if required.

In 1955 the AJ-flying Composite squadrons began to be re-designated as Heavy Attack (VAH, or 'HATRON'), with odd numbers on the east coast (VAH-5, -7, -9 and -11) and even on the Pacific (VAH-6). At this point the Savage's replacement was just around the corner. As for the AJ, it would be completely replaced in the VAH role by 1959, and largely unmissed.

DEVELOPING THE A3D

The requirement for what became the Skywarrior was laid out in 1948 when the US Navy stated a need for a jet-powered, carrier-based nuclear attack bomber. The new aircraft was already intended to replace the Savage in that role, even though the AJ was only then going through initial flight testing. The new design had to be able to fly a 2000-mile radius while carrying a 10,000-lb bomb to the target. Initial estimates at the US Navy's Bureau of Aeronautics said the new design might weigh up to 200,000 lbs, which would restrict it to only the planned 61,000-ton *United States* or later designs, and none of the World War 2-era carriers.

The perceived difficulty in meeting the request was demonstrated when at least five aviation companies declined to bid on the proposal. Indeed, only two, Douglas and Curtiss-Wright, submitted designs for what was now being called VAX(H). The Douglas team was, of course, headed by the company's Chief Engineer, Ed Heinemann, who was already well known for his work on the SBD Dauntless and AD Skyraider. Heinemann thought that the new aircraft could be smaller than most imagined. He felt that his team could come through with an aircraft that could operate safely off of 45,000-ton *Midway* class carriers, as well as the even smaller 29,000-ton *Essex* class vessels.

The size of the existing atomic weapon drove the entire design process, with a large bomb-bay necessarily shaping the company's approach. When all was said and done Douglas submitted a twin-engined jet with high-mounted swept wings that weighed no more than 34 tons when fully loaded. Its design's 'small' size initially created a lot of scepticism from the US Navy, but the aeroplane was soon ruled to be plausible. Heinemann's prescience was validated in April 1949 when the Department of Defense cancelled the *United States*. His efforts to make the design suitable for operation from smaller ships meant Douglas was still in business.

The new aircraft, designated the A3D-1, first flew on 16 September 1953, with Westinghouse J40 turbojets providing the thrust. The US Navy-developed J40 had been intended to be used in several new carrier aircraft, including the Douglas F4D Skyray and McDonnell F3H Demon. The engine instead went through severe developmental problems and was eventually cancelled, with Douglas quickly selecting the USAF-sponsored Pratt & Whitney J57 turbojet as a replacement.

What the US Navy got in the A3D-1 Skywarrior, as it was christened, was a 36,000-lb aircraft with high-mounted wings and a pair of J57-P-6 engines putting out roughly 9500 lbs of thrust each. Tough and reliable, the J57 was undoubtedly the most important US turbojet of the period – it powered the USAF's B-52, C-135, U-2, F-100, F-101 and F-102. The US Navy would use it in the F8U Crusader and F4D Skyray, along with the Skywarrior. The switch to the J57 proved to be a critical decision for the design, as the powerplant proved to be one of the type's strongest points throughout its career.

The cockpit of an A-3 was a mass of instruments, knobs and switches to the untrained, with the pilot's seat dominated by the control yoke. The centre console held the throttles, as well as the wing fold, flaps and gear controls. The B/N's seat featured controls for the ASB-1 radar. This photograph is of a Version, namely VA-3B BuNo 142672, and it was taken in 1980 after an Omega Navigation system has been fitted. Despite this, it accurately portrays the 'Whale's' flightdeck environment (*US Navy via Tailhook Association*)

The A3D-1's first flight in September 1953 was followed by a further three years of testing and troubleshooting before the type entered fleet service. Good to Ed Heinemann's promise, the aircraft could operate off the newly planned *Forrestal* class 'supercarriers', as well as existing *Midway* and *Essex* class boats that were modified with angled flightdecks and steam catapults.

The crew of three sat in a pressurised cockpit, with the pilot sitting on the left side with a yoke for control and the throttles mounted on a centre console. To his right, and offset slightly aft, was the seat of the bombardier/navigator (B/N). Early in the community this position was frequently occupied by an enlisted aircrewman, although by the early 1960s commissioned officers, rated as Naval Air Observers (NAOs), were taking over the job. The B/N operated the navigation/bombing radar – either an ASB-1 or ASB-7 depending on when the A3D was delivered. Both could provide an excellent picture for the jet's intended purpose. The B/N was also provided with an optical bombsight that featured a periscope exiting under the nose.

Sitting back-to-back with the pilot was the plane captain – normally an enlisted aircrewman. Also called the 'crewman/navigator', the plane captain controlled the aft-facing twin 20 mm cannon turret defensive armament. The guns had been specified by the US Navy over Heinemann's wishes, and they proved in practice to be of questionable effectiveness. The weapons were also hard to maintain. They were removed in the 1960-61 timeframe, with the back end being modified with a 'dovetail' (or 'duckbutt') fairing that could hold defensive Electronic Counter Measures (ECM).

In addition to the normal crew of three, a 'jump' seat was also fitted as a simple folding affair to the back wall for an additional rider.

Navigation was by radar and celestial means, with most A3D B/Ns taking a lot of pride in their proficiency with a sextant for taking sun shots. With their dedicated navigator and long legs, A3Ds would be used throughout their careers as pathfinders on long-range flights for smaller aircraft.

Entry into the aircraft was via a belly hatch that was located immediately behind the nose gear. The bombers had a second, inner door that closed flush with the cockpit floor – it also provided the cabin's pressure seal. The cockpit could be depressurised and the inner door opened to allow a crewman to enter the bomb-bay to arm a nuclear device or carry out some emergency procedures such as manual landing gear extension or resetting failed auxiliary systems.

Emergency egress was either via the belly or through a sliding overhead hatch while on deck or in the water. Bailing out of an A-3 involved pulling a handle on the side of the pilot's seat, which pneumatically blew down the inner and outer doors that then formed a continuous slide. Each crewman would then sequentially jump feet-first down the slide, with a barostatic release opening their parachute at 14,000 ft. Leaving the aircraft through the roof hatch while in flight was not recommended. In fact it was considered to be an absolutely last-ditch option only due to the likelihood of hitting the tail surfaces. Needless to say, successfully jumping out of an A-3 required time and altitude. NATOPS (Naval Air Training and Operating Procedures Standardization) recommended a minimum of 8000 ft and no more than 250 knots for a controlled bailout, but in reality conditions frequently required much less altitude and greater speeds.

The pilot, not surprisingly, had the hardest path to egress the aircraft. He had to stand up with his parachute and seat-pan survival kit and then rotate to his right while avoiding the centre console. Bailout at low altitudes was practically impossible, and it usually left the crew with no option other than to 'ride the aeroplane in', particularly if after a failed catapult shot on the carrier. An out-of-control condition would make safe egress all the more unlikely. Nonetheless, there were numerous successful escapes by 'Whale' crews over the years, some in situations that would otherwise defy belief.

The decision not to equip the A-3 series with ejection seats was not made lightly by the Douglas engineering team. When the aircraft was designed in the late 1940s there were no seats available that could save three men at low altitudes, particularly within the required weight limits. It would not be until delivery of the A2F Intruder a decade later that the US Navy had a fleet aircraft with two 'bang seats' installed. Ejection seat technology evolved quickly, however, and by the late 1950s requests from the fleet began to be submitted to retrofit the Skywarrior with the devices. Despite these calls the A-3 family retained its original egress design throughout its long life.

Although certainly not known for its aerobatic qualities, the A3D proved reasonably manoeuvrable in flight, and, in the hands of a smooth pilot, capable of rolls and inverted flight. Nuclear weapon delivery was via a modified wing-over manoeuvre in both day and night missions. The abilities of some 'drivers' notwithstanding, bank angle was limited 'by the book' to no-more than 120 degrees in the A-3B, and loops were forbidden, as was negative G and all inverted flight due to possible auxiliary drive

The first Skywarrior deployment was made by the 'Smoking Tigers' of VAH-1 in 1956 on the new 'supercarrier' USS *Forrestal* (CVA-59). Here, A3D-1 BuNo 135436/TB 6 flies over the ramp during carrier qualifications in September 1956. The 'Tare-Baker' tailcode was in honour of Capt Tommy Blackburn, the Commodore of Heavy Attack Wing One and famed F4U Corsair pilot from World War 2. In 1957 the squadron would be assigned the unique tailcode GH, although it would wear CVG-1's AB marking for its second major deployment. BuNo 135436 was the 44th A3D built (being delivered in February 1956), and it would not be retired until January 1968 (*US Navy*)

failure. The latter could in turn lead to the loss of hydraulic and electrical power at the worst possible time.

Maximum speed was 480 knots below 13,000 ft to a limit of 0.88 Mach to its ceiling of about 40,000 ft. Maximum G-loading was 2.5 to 4.3, depending on conditions and weight.

The A-3B weighed 43,000 lbs empty, a maximum catapult shot was 73,000 lbs and landing weight for the boat was 50,000 lbs. In 1959 an A3D-2 was launched from USS *Saratoga* (CVA-60) at a staggering gross weight of 84,000 lbs, making it the heaviest aircraft to ever be catapulted from a carrier flightdeck. The A-3 used a bridle to hook up to the catapult shuttle – the type's longevity made it the last fleet aircraft to use the system, long after the nose-tow launch system had been adopted. Only the T-2C Buckeye, used in training command, outlasted the A-3 in American use of that carrier launch method.

Another significant change to the airframe introduced deep in production was the Cambered Leading Edge Wing (CLE or 'CLEO'). The CLE sought to reduce the approach speed of the type by slightly increasing the curvature, or camber, of the wing inboard of the engines. While all Skywarriors had aerodynamic leading edge slats located outboard of the engine nacelles, the CLE had them between the engines and fuselage. Introduced on the 178th airframe (A-3B BuNo 142650) in December 1958, only 67 'Whales' would get the feature, which reduced landing speeds by two to three knots. The original design became known as the 'Basic Wing', and aircrew had to account for the differences between the two designs when computing things like takeoff and landing characteristics.

INTO THE FLEET

The first squadron to receive the Skywarrior was Heavy Attack Squadron One (VAH-1), newly established on 1 November 1955 at NAS Jacksonville, Florida. Behind it was VAH-3, formed from VP-34 on

15 June 1956. Both units received new A3D-1s and prepared for operations. VAH-1 went to sea first, joining CVG-1 onboard *Forrestal* for work-ups in October 1956. A Mediterranean deployment followed in January 1957, thus setting the pattern for several years to come. The 'Sea Dragons' of VAH-3 followed, embarking nine A3D-1s onboard USS *Franklin D Roosevelt* (CVA-42) and heading to the Mediterranean as part of CVG-17 in July 1957.

As can be expected, the US Navy heavily publicised its new aircraft. Douglas followed suit, featuring it in a promotional film titled 'Jet Bombers at Sea' that expounded on the dramatic, new capability the type provided the fleet. Yet these early deployments also highlighted areas where the design needed improvement before it could be fully accepted for fleet duty. Ultimately, VAH-1 and VAH-3 were the only two squadrons that deployed with the 'Dash One' Skywarrior, which was, in effect, a prototype design with a good number of bugs that needed to be worked out. Areas that needed rectifying included the provision of stronger mountings for the auxiliaries, the fitting of engines with greater power and, after several window-panel blow-outs at high altitudes, more robust canopy frames.

Both units had issues with maintenance as they determined what level of parts support was needed to keep the aircraft operational. VAH-1's serviceability problems led to the following story involving the unit's commanding officer. Having supposedly been asked by a visitor if his unit had ever managed to get all 12 of its aircraft airborne at the same time, his somewhat sarcastic response was reported to be 'Yeah, when they're all up on jacks in the hangar bay'.

His sarcasm only slightly covered multiple ongoing problems in the wake of the fleet introduction of the type. Near the top of major concerns were secondary power sections. The aircraft's auxiliaries were powered by hot bleed-air tapped off the engines and then routed via ducting up through the engine pylons and the wings to the fuselage, where it then went to a compartment located underneath the cockpit. The high-pressure air then spun a pair of Air Turbine Motors (ATMs, also called Auxiliary Drive Units or ADUs), which each in turn ran an electrical generator and hydraulic pump. The long piping carrying very hot air was always a major concern for A-3 crews, as any leak could quickly cause a tremendous amount of damage or even start a fire.

At the first sign of any problems – usually an ATM Fire light on the console – the pilot would secure the bleed air in that line through a valve at the engine. The aircraft could operate fine on only half of the system. If both had to be shut down the bombers carried an emergency battery system for electrical power and, with no hydraulics, the pilot would pull a handle that would revert the flight control system to fully manual, resulting in an aircraft that, although flyable, was very sluggish and took two strong arms to fly. This mechanical system was very similar to what was installed in the A4D, but there was a big difference in manually flying a 9500-lb Skyhawk and a 50,000-lb Skywarrior.

More troubling to senior officers was a frighteningly high initial loss rate, and concerns that the some of the aircraft's pilots might not be up to flying it around the carrier. Most of the initial cadre of Naval Aviators assigned to A3D units had come from the Patrol (VP) community, who,

The learning curve for operating A3Ds around the carrier was steep, both in terms of men and equipment. No fewer than 27 Skywarriors were lost prior to 1960 – eight of these were during carrier landings, with 13 men being killed. One of the more tragic accidents occurred on 26 September 1957 when Cdr Paul Wilson, skipper of VAH-1, suffered a ramp strike on *Forrestal* in BuNo 135417/AB 7. The aircraft, its back broken, slid down the flightdeck and crashed into the Atlantic streaming fire. All three onboard were killed, as was one flightdeck crewman who was hit by debris. Between 1955 and 1988 roughly 42 per cent of all Skywarrior production was lost in accidents or in combat, with aircrew suffering a staggering 67 per cent mortality rate in these incidents (*US Navy*)

while familiar with multi-engined, multi-crew aircraft, typically had only limited experience around the boat, with some senior officers having only a fraction of the arrested landings in their logbooks that would be considered 'normal' for career carrier aviators of their rank.

Crashes became all too frequent, and some grimly notable. In 1957 – the first full year of fleet duty – there were seven major accidents, three of which were spectacular carrier landing mishaps that killed nine men, including ramp strikes that took the lives of senior officers in both VAH-1 and VAH-2. Photographs of their burning aircraft sliding down the flightdeck clearly showed the doomed crew riding a fireball with no means of escape. Images like these were seared into the minds of many inside and out of the community.

Once deployments started it was quickly obvious that the Heavy Attack community was having serious problems fitting in with normal carrier operations. After several years of dealing with the less-than-satisfactory AJ Savage and its issues, many had adopted a 'wait and see' attitude for the new jet bomber from Douglas. For some it was too much, as exemplified by Commander, Sixth Fleet, Vice Admiral Charles R 'Cat' Brown, who sent a blunt message to the Pentagon stating that VAH units should be removed from the carriers and that the whole concept of Heavy Attack should be re-evaluated, particularly as single-seat jets like the F2H Banshee and new A4D Skyhawk were now able to deliver an improved series of smaller nuclear weapons.

Needless to say, the issue was serious. The focus again turned to the pilots who were being assigned to the new jet, as it was maintained that there were not enough carrier-experienced aviators in the community. While some of the former VP pilots flourished (including Lt Ed Mitchell,

15

who made two deployments with VAH-2, joined NASA in 1966 and became the sixth man to walk on the Moon as a member of Apollo XIV in February 1971), many did not. Statistics quietly circulated at high levels showed that among the six squadrons at NAS Sanford, Florida, none of the critical CO/XO/Operations Officer jobs were held by men with jet carrier experience, and several of them had had no carrier time of any sort prior to assignment to A3Ds.

The US Navy quickly decided that it had to retain the capability that the Skywarrior promised and find a way to make it work. The initial solution dealt with leadership, with new Wing Commodores like Capts James D 'Jig Dog' Ramage at Sanford and William 'Bush' Bringle at NAS Whidbey Island, in Washington State, stressing professional carrier airmanship and the implementation of strict training standards. They also demanded, and got, an influx of mid-grade jet-experienced carrier pilots injected into the community (as, frequently stated, 'kicking and screaming') to provide a core of boat-experienced operators.

Other late 1950s developments helped, including the new RAG (Replacement Air Group) system, with VAH-3 being pulled from fleet duty after only one deployment and being converted to a training squadron at Sanford to instruct new aircrew and maintenance personnel in the aircraft.

Additional significant factors included the adoption of improved carrier landing systems, such as the Fresnel Lens, and adoption of standardised procedures introduced through the new NATOPS programme. The latter actually took several years to take hold, as many older pilots viewed normalised procedures and training as an affront to their abilities as aviators – as one high-time A-3 pilot put it, 'NATOPS was written by men who were afraid to fly'. Nonetheless, the programme was adopted US Navy-wide and eventually became written in stone (and blood, according to its supporters).

While VAH-1 and VAH-3 were sorting out the 'Dash One's' myriad problems, Heavy Attack Wing One (HATWING One) was converting

A pair of HATWING One A3D-1s fly over central Florida in this photograph, which was taken in the late 1958/early 1959 timeframe. Both aircraft wear unique squadron codes. GL 404 (BuNo 135420) is from VAH-7 'Go-Devils', which never made a complete deployment in Skywarriors before converting to A3J Vigilantes. Trailing is GJ 210 (BuNo 135415), from VAH-3. The 'Sea Dragons' made only one deployment before becoming the wing's training squadron (*US Navy via Rich Dann*)

Typical of the early leadership in the Heavy Attack community was Cdr Art Irish, the first CO of VAH-2. A patrol pilot, Irish was CO of VP-29 (a P2V Neptune squadron) when it was re-designated VAH-2 and moved to North Island to become the Pacific Fleet's first A3D unit on 1 November 1955. He is shown here looking dapper in a set of Aviation Greens in a suitable official pose taken in May 1956 with a Skywarrior model notably displayed on his desk (*US Navy*)

its AJ force at Sanford, with VAH-5, -7, -9 and -11 all getting the new A3D-2. The 'Dash Two' was a true production aircraft, with significant improvements over the A3D-1. It had more powerful J57-P-10 engines, with 500 lbs more thrust on each side, as well as greater G-loading available (up to 3.4 now), provisions for fitment of a bomb-bay fuel tank and tanker package and other system improvements.

By the end of the third and fourth VAH Mediterranean cruises (performed in 1958 by VAH-9 and VAH-5, respectively) things had improved to such a degree that Vice Admiral Brown sent out a widely disseminated retraction of his previous message. In it he plainly stated that he had been wrong, and that 'eating crow isn't hard when it tastes like filet mignon'.

The two NAS Jacksonville-based units moved to Sanford in mid-1959, with the result that HATWING One would subsequently have five A3D-2 squadrons deploying to the Mediterranean on *Midway* and *Forrestal* class carriers. Basing all aircraft of a like type at one airfield was still unusual for the US Navy, which traditionally kept its carrier air groups united at various bases, no matter what type of aircraft they flew. The A3D community practically led the way in this 'type basing' concept, which the rest of the service would soon follow.

AIRPAC AND WHIDBEY ISLAND

Out West, Commander, Naval Air Forces Pacific (AirPac) had elected to base its new Heavy Attack community at NAS Whidbey Island. Located in Island County, some two hours driving time north of Seattle, Whidbey was probably the most remote major facility in the US Navy.

The first A3D delivered to the Pacific
Fleet was BuNo 135440/BF 1, a 'Dash
One' accepted by VAH-2 CO Art Irish
at Los Angeles Airport on 30 April
1956. The squadron would fly A3D-1s
for only a short period before getting
A3D-2s. VAH-2's unit tailcode became
ZA in 1957. BuNo 135440 would be
lost while flying with VAH-1 in
August 1960, with one crewman
being killed (*Douglas*)

Located near the Dutch-influenced town of Oak Harbor, Whidbey had originally been opened as an auxiliary field for NAS Seattle during World War 2, but its location and growth potential led to its expansion through the mid to late 1950s. While the airfield was initially home to VP units only, the US Navy eventually commissioned the building of two new 8000 ft runways to handle jets and establish its Pacific Fleet A3D community there as well.

Heavy Attack Wing Two (HATWING Two) had been formed at NAS North Island, California, to oversee the Pacific Fleet's AJs. With its squadrons being even-numbered, VAH-6 still had Savages when VAH-2 was established on 1 November 1955 from VP-29 to become the first Pacific Fleet A3D outfit. VAH-2, under Cdr Art Irish, received its initial A3D-1 in April 1956 and, subsequently, new A3D-2s. In July 1957 the squadron made the first deployment for the type in the Pacific theatre, with Detachment N taking three A3D-2s onboard USS *Bon Homme Richard* (CVA-31) with CVG-5 for a WestPac cruise. Detachment M followed in September aboard USS *Ticonderoga* (CVA-14) as part of CVG-9.

The use of the 'small deck' modified *Essex* class carriers became a Pacific Fleet hallmark as it had, unlike its Atlantic equivalent in 1957, no 'supercarriers' assigned. The 'Bonnie Dick' was one of six *Essex* class vessels modified under the SCB27C/125 programme with steam catapults, angled flightdecks and other improvements that would allow them to operate high-performance jet aircraft. Five of these ships (along with the one-of-a-kind USS *Oriskany* (CVA-34), with its unique SCB27A/125A configuration) would become the stuff of legends in the coming war in Vietnam. The Atlantic Fleet would never deploy Skywarriors to the Mediterranean with their few counterparts.

AirPac's deployment plan initially involved sending detachments of three A3D-2s with the *Essex* class ships, full-strength squadrons of nine to eleven jets on the *Midway* class carriers and 12 when *Forrestal* class flightdecks arrived in-theatre.

VAH-2 moved to Whidbey Island in December 1957, along with the HATWING. The second Pacific unit, VAH-4, had been formed from VP-57 on 1 July 1956, and it retained P2V Neptunes until its first Skywarrior arrived that December. Self-styled as the 'Four-Runners', the squadron was followed by the 'Fireballers' of VAH-8, which was established on 1 May 1957. The 'Fleurs' of VAH-6 (AirPac's AJ Savage unit) transferred to Whidbey in January 1958 without aircraft, thus becoming the base's third A3D outfit.

By the start of 1960 Whidbey's four squadrons were servicing all of the Pacific Fleet CVAs, with VAH-2 now embarking as a complete squadron onboard USS *Coral Sea* (CVA-43) with CVG-15, VAH-8 assigned to *Midway* with CVG-2 and VAH-6 taking 12 aircraft onboard the fleet's newly arrived 'supercarrier' USS *Ranger* (CVA-61) as part of CVG-9. VAH-4 was unique in that it would never deploy as a full squadron, but was now the 'small deck' modernised-*Essex* specialist, supplying the carrier air groups that deployed in USS *Lexington* (CVA-16), USS *Hancock* (CVA-19), *Bon Homme Richard*, *Ticonderoga* and *Oriskany*.

Whidbey was also home to VAH-123, which operated as the west coast A3D training squadron. The 'Professionals' had been established on 29 June 1959 out of the former Heavy Attack Training Unit, Pacific Fleet (HATUPAC). Becoming a member of the AirPac RAG, RCVG-12, VAH-123's inventory would, for a time, include P2V-3Bs and F9F-8Ts – the Neptunes for B/N training and the Cougars for jet pilot transition and instrument training. New eight-seat A3D-2T B/N trainers would arrive in 1962, while A3D-1s were used for pilot instruction through to 1963, when they were replaced by A3D-2/A-3Bs.

VAH-4's BuNo 138913/ZB 3 exemplifies early A3D-2 deployments to WestPac, as brownshirts remove the jury struts from the wing prior to launching from *Hancock* in 1958. The aircraft wears HATWING Two's insignia under the cockpit. BuNo 138913 was lost on 5 May 1959 when an arrestor cable parted on recovery aboard *Lexington*. All three crew members were rescued (*US Navy via Rich Dann*)

Heavy Attack Wing Two was disestablished at Whidbey on 1 July 1959, with its function being taken over by Commander, Fleet Air Whidbey (COMFAIRWHIDBEY), who also controlled the remaining P2V squadrons at the base.

A fifth Pacific Fleet squadron was established on 1 May 1961 in the form of VAH-10. The newest unit was intended for the new *Kitty Hawk* class carrier USS *Constellation* (CVA-64), and it joined CVG-13 in the Caribbean for the ship's shakedown cruise. Although they had initially called themselves the 'Strikers', the carrier air group started referring to VAH-10 as 'those Vikings from the cold northwest', and the Nordic title stuck.

Whidbey's last A3D squadron arrived in October 1961 as VAH-13 reported onboard with the transfer of USS *Kitty Hawk* (CVA-63) to the Pacific Fleet. Called the 'Bats', with an insignia based on the Bacardi rum logo, VAH-13 would only make two WestPac deployments with the 'Hawk' and CVG-11 before moving back to sunny Florida for transition to another aircraft.

HIGH TIDE

The last of 283 Skywarriors was delivered by Douglas in January 1961, with the 'high water mark' of the Skywarrior population being reached in mid-1961 with 227 airframes in service. Little noted was that more than 40 aircraft had already been lost in accidents.

In May 1962 the US Navy re-designated its aircraft, with the A3D-1 becoming the A-3A and the A3D-2 the A-3B.

Up to now the jet's primary mission had been nuclear deterrence, with squadrons typically keeping one or two aircraft armed with a 'special weapon' and available for launch in the hangar bay, which was in turn guarded by US Marine Corps personnel. Tanking and conventional

VAH-6 'Fluers' parades its entire squadron of 12 A3D-2s (in correct Modex order) at a sunny NAS Whidbey Island in August 1961, the jets taxiing past aircraft from VAH-4 (ZB code) and VAH-123 (NJ). Each aircraft has a COMFAIRWHIDBEY 'Bomber Stream' competition flag flying from its upper hatch, the squadron having won the event for five successive months in 1961. VAH-6, assigned to CVG-9 in *Ranger* at that time, transferred to Sanford for RA-5C conversion prior to the Vietnam War. The last aircraft, NG 12 (BuNo 147662) was only ten months old at the time of this photograph. It went missing with its crew of three on 13 November 1962 while flying a mission off *Ranger* (*US Navy*)

One of designer Ed Heinemann's proudest achievements with the Skywarrior was that it could operate off of *Essex* class carriers modified with steam catapults and angled flightdecks. This engineering feat paid off when 'Whale' units assigned to the Pacific Fleet made their first of several deployments on the smaller-deck vessels. This is USS *Bon Homme Richard* (CVA 31) underway in 1961 with 27 aircraft on deck of the 69 then assigned to CVG-19. Visible in this aerial photograph are Skyhawks, Demons and Skyraiders, as well as solitary examples of the Crusader and WF-2 'Willy Fudd'. The amount of space required for the pair of VAH-4 Det Echo A3D-2s is obvious. Heavy Four specialised in supplying detachments to modified *Essex* class ships for several years. (*US Navy via the Tailhook Association*)

A typical three-man Skywarrior crew briefs a flight onboard *Bon Homme Richard* in 1961. On the right is B/N Lt(jg) Lyle Bull, in the middle is VAH-4 Det E's OinC, Lt Cdr Charlie Cates, and to the left is the crewman, identified as PO Corbaugh. Bull would later move to Intruders, be awarded a Navy Cross for combat in Vietnam and reach the rank of rear admiral. Cates would command VAH-8 and be killed after ejecting from an A-7B on the runway at NAF Naha, Okinawa, on 18 August 1969 while serving as CAG of CVW-16, embarked in CVA-14 (*US Navy via Rear Admiral Lyle Bull*)

bombing were also practised, but they were not the primary reason for their existence.

According to one experienced pilot, 'the "special weapon" delivery technique was to run in at very low altitude – down among the short-legged sheep – at 520 knots. When the B/N had the target on radar he'd command a pull-up, which was done at 2.5Gs. You'd make sure the throttles were fully forward – most aeroplanes could do 520 knots on the deck at less than military thrust – and pitch to 60 degrees nose up. The bomb-bay doors opened, the bomb rake extended, the weapon released and the doors closed. This all took place in about one second. You'd roll the aircraft 120 degrees, still at 2.5Gs, and decrease the angle-of-bank to 90 degrees as the nose went through the horizon as you continued your turn in the opposite direction to avoid the blast'.

The rapid rise in the submarine-launched Polaris missile force spelled the eventual end of the A-3 deterrence mission, as did the introduction of a replacement platform, the North American A3J (A-5A post 1962)

Vigilante. The latter aircraft was a 'stone-cold beauty' as well as being both big and very fast. The US Navy wasted no time in replacing A3Ds at Sanford with A3Js, and HATWING One started transitioning units to the new mount, with Fleet Replacement Squadron VAH-3 getting its first aircraft in June 1961. VAH-1 followed, making its first deployment – to the Mediterranean – with the A-5A onboard USS *Independence* (CVA-62) as part of CVG-7 in 1963.

The 'Vigi' (as well covered in 'Boom' Powell's volume *Osprey Combat Aircraft 51 – RA-5C Vigilante Units in Combat*) was well received in the A3D community as many viewed it as a great step forward. Page Carter, an A3D B/N at Sanford during this period stated that 'at least the A3J gave you a chance to get home after delivering your weapon. We all figured the A3D was pretty much a one-way mission'.

Conversion of the Sanford wing was quick, even after the nuclear-bombing mission of the A3J had morphed into photo-reconnaissance with the RA-5C as Heavy Photo-Reconnaissance units (RVAH). By the start of the Vietnam War VAH-11 was the only squadron still flying the A-3B out of Sanford, and it too would get 'Vigis' in 1966.

By 1965 the centre of the A-3 universe was Whidbey Island, with four deploying squadrons (VAH-2, -4, -8 and -10). Two other units (VAH-6 and -13) had by then moved to Sanford to become RVAH squadrons. VAH-123 was now the only A-3 RAG, its east coast counterpart now training Vigilante crews. The four squadrons located in the Pacific Northwest would now carry Heavy Attack into the start of the war in Vietnam.

Five A-3Bs from the 'Checkertails' of VAH-11 Det 8 prepare for launch from *Forrestal* in the spring of 1964. With the remainder of the squadron assigned to CVW-1 *Franklin D Roosevelt*, Det 8 continued to carry its 'home' tailcodes while working with CVW-8. Aircraft from the latter air wing visible in this photograph are A-4Es (VA-81), RF-8As (VFP-62), A-1Hs (VA-85) and a single F-4B (VF-74). VA-85 would actually start transition to A-6As shortly thereafter, while Heavy Eleven, the last Sanford-based A-3B squadron, would get RA-5Cs in mid-1966 (*US Navy via Tailhook Association and Angelo Romano*)

WHIDBEY – BOMBING AND TANKING

On 2 August 1964 US carrier aviation publicly entered the war in Vietnam as aircraft launched from the flightdeck of *Ticonderoga* attacked North Vietnamese patrol boats in defence of the destroyer USS *Maddox* (DD-731) in what became known as the Gulf of Tonkin Incident. Onboard 'Tico' was Lt Cdr D L Jensen's VAH-4 Det B, with a trio of A-3Bs assigned to Carrier Air Wing (CVW) Five. Nearby was USS *Constellation* (CVA-64) with a complete squadron of 12 'Whales' in the form of the 'Vikings' of VAH-10, led by Cdr Tyler Dedman.

Over the next nine years the United States would conduct open warfare against North Vietnam, with Naval Aviation being one of the primary weapons used to protect its South Vietnamese ally from what was regarded as naked communist aggression.

Practically every attack aircraft carrier (CVA) that fought in Vietnam had A-3s in some form embarked, either as bombers, tankers or in the photo and electronic reconnaissance roles. At least 62 separate cruises were conducted by the bomber/tanker units alone, running from small three-aircraft detachments to complete twelve-aircraft squadrons. Sixteen different attack carriers operated Skywarriors during the war, with only USS *Intrepid* (CVS-11, functioning as a CVA) and *Saratoga* not deploying

A Heavy Four Det B A-3B off *Ticonderoga* leads a pair of VA-56 A-4Es in early 1964. The 'Whale' has neither a refuelling probe nor tanker package (*US Navy via Peter Mersky*)

with them. The price for this constant rotation of ships, squadrons and men to the war zone would be notable, as six Skywarriors were lost in combat, 12 more destroyed operationally in theatre and 35 crew killed.

'WHALE' AS A BOMBER

Although nuclear strike had long been its primary mission, conventional bombing was not unknown in the A-3 community as the aircraft could carry up to 8000 lbs of ordnance internally, being limited by carriage issues more than mass. Weapons diagrams showed 13 different combinations of bombs and mines that could be carried, with typical loads without a tanker package being 12 high drag or six Mk 82 low drag 500-lb bombs – fewer of the latter weapon could be carried due to attachment point configuration and bomb length.

VAH-2 would be the first Skywarrior unit to actually drop bombs in combat. A split squadron, it had Det M flying three aircraft under Cdr D E Brandenburg in *Ranger* with CVW-9. Deploying in August 1964, it would return home the following May. The bulk of the unit (nine aircraft) joined CVW-15 embarked in *Coral Sea*, which left San Francisco in December 1964 for what would be an almost 11-month deployment.

The official squadron history states that Det M delivered ordnance in 1964, but details are not provided. Better recorded is the 29 March 1965

VAH-10 had 12 bombers onboard *Constellation* during the Gulf of Tonkin incident, becoming one of the first two A-3B squadrons to be involved in the new war. BuNo 142632/NK 109 displays the look of a straight bomber in 1964 at NAS North Island, California (*Bill Swisher via Tailhook Association*)

VAH-2 entered the war in August 1964 with Det M and three A-3Bs embarked in *Ranger*, the balance of the squadron – nine aircraft – arriving in-theatre onboard *Coral Sea* four months later. It was during these two cruises that the 'Royal Rampants' became the first Skywarrior squadron to drop bombs in anger. ZA 692, a tanker-configured A-3B from Det A, is shown here ashore during CVA-43's 1966-67 combat deployment. It has a candy-striped refuelling probe and carries the unit's unique tailcode (*via Rich Dann*)

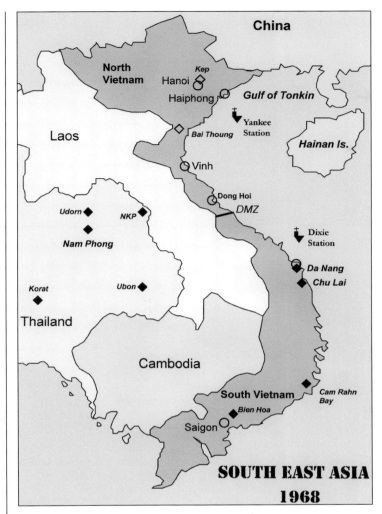

China

North Vietnam

Kep

Hanoi

Haiphong

Gulf of Tonkin

Hainan Is.

Bai Thoung

Yankee Station

Laos

Vinh

Dong Hoi

DMZ

Udorn

NKP

Nam Phong

Dixie Station

Korat

Ubon

Da Nang

Chu Lai

Thailand

Cambodia

South Vietnam

Cam Rahn Bay

Bien Hoa

Saigon

SOUTH EAST ASIA 1968

attack by VAH-2 aircraft off *Coral Sea*. Squadron commander Cdr Robert de Lorenzi led six bombers on a night radar-directed straight-path strike on three separate points on Bach Long Vi Island, located in the middle of the Gulf of Tonkin. Their targets were a headquarters building for a small garrison, their barracks and a radar site that was believed to be providing information on US Navy activities. Twelve tons of bombs – a mix of 500 and 1000 'pounders' – were dropped, with at least two of the targets being reported as destroyed.

Among the squadron members was Lt(jg) Dick Toft, a young B/N. He would later say that they dropped a lot of old M-series 'high drag' bombs during the cruise, many of which had been in storage since the Korean War. 'The air wing preferred that we carry the box-fin bombs in our bomb-bay and let the A-4s get the (low drag) Mk 82s, if they were available. You could see on preflight that many (of the older weapons) were corroded and possessed questionable ballistic characteristics. You never really knew if the fins would stay on or where the ordnance would go when it left the aircraft'.

During the course of the 331-day deployment (164 of which were 'on the line' in combat) the 'Royal Rampants' flew 4900 hours, transferred more than four million pounds of fuel and dropped in excess of 400,000 lbs of bombs. The unit was also credited with saving 17 aircraft from CVW-15 through tanking.

During 1966-67 Skywarrior detachments rolled through the theatre, and most delivered ordnance as part of their duties. The lack of radar-significant targets in the largely agrarian north, as well as concerns for the survivability of the 'Whale' in the face of rapidly improving communist defences, quickly led to the A-3 undertaking missions in the south, as well as along the Ho Chi Minh Trail.

How to use the aircraft though was the question, as level delivery with the radar or even optical sight was impractical in the jungles of the south or when friendly troops were nearby. The answer was the adoption of dive-bombing, which, while not completely new to the community, was not widely practiced because the aircraft did not have a visual bombsight installed for the pilot. US Navy ingenuity initially led to the use of simple

An obviously re-touched photograph that shows a tanker-equipped A-3B of VAH-8 in a 30-degree dive over South Vietnam. The bomb-bay and speed brakes are open and the bomb rake has been deployed as an M-series box-fin bomb heads for the jungle. BuNo 147649 would be rebuilt as an EKA-3B in October 1967 and lost in a mishap with VAQ-130 while flying from Da Nang on 18 June 1971, killing all three crewmen (*US Navy via Angelo Romano*)

Crews manning VAH-8 A-3s await the signal to start on the deck of *Midway* during the 1965 deployment. Both aircraft still have their wing struts installed and are equipped with Cambered Leading Edge wings, as evidenced by the wing slats inboard of the engines. The jet closest to the camera is carrying a crew of four, with one man standing in the upper hatch. BuNo 147667 was the next-to-last, and 282nd, A-3 built. Aircraft from VF-21, VA-22 and VA-23 are shown lining CVA-41's port side (*US Navy via Rich Dann*)

grease-pencil markings on the windscreen, or referencing the nose refuelling probe as an aiming point.

With the war raging, the carriers continued their cycle, with some ships and air wings returning to theatre after only six months, or less, at home. The fourth, and last, Whidbey-based 'Whale' unit to make an appearance in the combat zone was VAH-8 'Fireballers', which arrived with eight aircraft as part of CVW-2 embarked in *Midway* in March 1965 – the squadron performed both bombing and tanking missions whilst in Southeast Asia. This proved to be the last time that an A-3 squadron would deploy with as many as nine aircraft, as subsequent deployments were normally made with five jets on larger decks and three on the '27C' hulls.

Among the 'Fireballer' pilots was Lt Cdr Bill Barnes, a former NAVCAD (Naval Aviation Cadet) who had seen combat in F9F-5 Panthers with VF-53 in Korea as an ensign. A notably blunt and self-assured individual, Barnes had left the service after Korea and obtained degrees from the University of Illinois and Cornell, before working for the Borg-Warner

A Skywarrior crew from VAH-10 conducts pre-flight checks on the nose of their aircraft on board CVA-64 in what may be a staged photograph from 1964-65. The man to the left appears to be connecting the nose gear scissors, which was required to be disconnected for towing. All three aviators wear standard survival gear for the early-war period, including a survival knife, 0.38-cal special revolver and ammunition, all over orange flightsuits and squadron-unique caps. No anti-G suits are worn. The large fairing under the nose covers the B/N's bombsight – it would be moved aft prior to use so as to uncover the optical sight (*US Navy via Peter Mersky*)

Corporation. Barnes eventually 'became bored' and returned to the US Navy, being assigned to A-3s. He joined the squadron during cruise and went right to work as the senior O-4 (Lieutenant Commander) in the outfit;

'I liked the Skipper, but the XO and I didn't get along. That didn't matter though as I was happy to be there. The "Whale" was a beautiful, bird, and I ended up with more than 2500 hours in the type. We had both basic- and CLE-winged aircraft – the basics were generally used as bombers while the "Cleos" usually had the tanker packages. A number of our aircraft were always on the beach at Cubi in order to provide more room on the flightdeck, although we still flew a lot of missions out of both locations. Bombing was either level with radar delivery or visual dive, typically on marshalling yards and barracks, all in lightly defended areas. We got pretty good at it actually.'

Among the more notable flights for VAH-8 was providing tanking for the first US Navy MiG killers of the war when VF-21 Phantom IIs splashed a pair of North Vietnamese fighters on 17 June.

The cockpit of an unidentified A-3 in-flight. The pilot is to the left, while the crewman pointing is actually between the pilot and B/N – he is probably occupying the fold-down jump seat that was used during takeoff and landing. 'Whale' crews frequently flew with their oxygen masks off, using boom mikes for communication. The aircraft's throttles are visible in the centre, while the inverted 'mushroom' switch under the 'wet' compass deployed the drag chute (*US Navy via Peter Mersky*)

Whidbey's VAH-123 was the community's training squadron ('RAG') until 1971, when VAQ-130 took over. The 'Professionals' used A-3As, (K)A-3Bs and TA-3Bs for the job. Carrier qualification was a critical part of the syllabus – here, A-3B NJ 306 accelerates after a touch-and-go on an unidentified flightdeck (*US Navy*)

The 'Four-Runners' of VAH-4 had been in the war at the start, the unit being heavily involved supporting detachments that quickly deployed in 1965 onboard *Oriskany* and *Hancock*. In May of that year the squadron placed its first unit aboard a 'supercarrier' when Det 62 joined Norfolk-based *Independence* for what would prove to be the ship's only visit to the war zone. The initial Officer-in-Charge (OinC) during the cruise, Bob Belter, was a Heavy Attack veteran who had received his wings in 1950, with his first orders as a P2V 'driver' to VP-5 at Jacksonville.

After a tour as an instrument flight instructor Belter was ordered to VC-6, where he learned to fly the AJ-2 in a carrier environment. Belter actually enjoyed the Savage, calling it a 'Big, Boxy SOB, but amazingly fast at altitude when all three engines were going'. He made AJ cruises in USS *Bennington* (CVA-20) and USS *Kearsarge* (CVA-33) and eventually went through jet transition to join the growing A3D community at Whidbey. After conversion to the A3D-1 at HATUPAC, he immediately became an instructor in the type, staying at Whidbey until ordered to Naval Postgraduate School in Monterey, California. Belter eventually returned in Whidbey and joined VAH-4, making its 1964 WestPac in *Bon Homme Richard* as an OinC of Det E.

Among the more unusual jobs given to his det was to fly a 'Whale' to Japan to collect the first combat pay for the ship's crew. Belter returned with four large bags of money and an ensign supply officer on his first flight. They trapped and were met by the ship's Supply Officer, along with a group of armed Marines, to pick up the cash.

Once back home turnaround was quick, and as previously noted, Belter subsequently became OinC of Det 62, which took three A-3Bs aboard 'Indy'. This cruise would include both tanking and bombing. Belter recalled that, without a bombsight, pilots learned to use the tip of the refuelling probe as a reference point for delivering ordnance. Drops using this method required precise pilot applications, with consistent airspeed, dive angle and release altitudes being necessary to put bombs close to where the Forward Air Controllers (FAC) wanted them. Dive-bombing typically started at 8000 ft to 10,000 ft, with pull-out initiated at 3000 ft above the terrain so as to avoid light anti-aircraft fire and prevent airframe over-stress. Nonetheless, actual effects against indistinct targets were frequently hard to determine. As Belter put it, 'We had no problem hitting the jungle'.

Other strikes were flown with air wing A-4s, frequently with the Skyhawks dropping on command from the 'Whale'. 'We did well', Belter explained. 'The first CVW-7 ordnance delivered on arrival was from my A-3B on an in-country warm-up that dropped 6000 lbs (three Mk 84s) for a FAC in South Vietnam. No bombsight, just the "aiming pole" [refuelling probe] and "Kentucky windage". Not the way to fight a war! We also did some work up north one night, making a radar strike on Ham-Rong port just above Thanh Hoa, with A-4s on our wing. We took some AAA on that one but all the jets got back to the carrier okay. Ultimately, we still ended up doing about four tanker flights for every bomber sortie, as that's what CAG wanted'.

Along with its A-3s and A-4s, CVW-7 had the first A-6 Intruder squadron in-theatre as well. VA-75 introduced what was soon called 'medium attack' to Naval Aviation, its Intruders providing both greater bomb tonnage and improved survivability than the 'Whale'. It was, in reality, the real future of US carrier strike power.

Belter would go on to serve as an Aviation Engineering Duty Officer (AEDO) at Patuxent River and fly the test programme for the EKA-3B, as well as field trials for the short-lived F-111B. He would eventually take over the Navy office at the Grumman plant on Long Island and retire with the rank of captain.

A close-up of a cockpit section of a VAH-4 Det L/31 A-3B onboard *Bon Homme Richard* in 1967. The upper hatch is slid full aft and there are four men onboard, the gentleman in the orange flight suit apparently intending to use the fold-down 'jump seat' on the aft cockpit wall. This photograph also shows how the B/N's seat was offset aft from the pilot's. The white tape antenna in the aft quarter panel is associated with the ARN-59 navigation system (*John Stewart via Peter Mersky*)

Another of the early 'Whale' bomber pilots was Tad Bingham, a native of Logan, Utah. Bingham had flown his first tour in F11F Tiger day fighters with VF-191. After a stint ashore he had requested assignment to the new F4H Phantom II and was ordered to A3Ds instead, ending up with VAH-13 at Whidbey. In spite of the tremendous change in aircraft, Bingham quickly fell in love with the 'Whale', and the people associated with it. After a full peacetime cruise with the 'Bats' he was serving with COMFAIRWHIDBEY (Commander, Fleet Air Whidbey) in 1965 when word came that VAH-4 Det G onboard *Oriskany* had lost an aircraft.

When the call went out that the det needed a new pilot Bingham volunteered, heading directly to the Gulf of Tonkin with a replacement jet. He made the rest of the cruise and became adept at 30-degree dive-bombing with the A-3B;

'We ended up with four aircraft, although only one carried a tanker package – the rest were used for bombing. The lack of a real bombsight was a concern, so some of our enlisted men were able to scrounge sights out of A-1s that they managed to mount onto the glare shield. With a little practice we got pretty good with this system, dropping single bombs under the control of a FAC.'

Bingham would soon leave the regular US Navy and in time fly KA-3Bs with the Reserves at Alameda.

Subsequent VAH-4 dets would also use jury-rigged A-4 sights as well. Since the mounts were never approved by the Bureau of Aeronautics, they would have to be removed upon the A-3s' return to the US, yet they did the job.

VAH-4 Det Bravo, flying off *Bon Homme Richard* with CVW-5 in 1966, logged 180 bombing missions that saw it expend 490,000 lbs of ordnance. The versatility of the det's 'Whales' during this deployment was described in an article published in the 4 March edition of the Whidbey Island base paper *Propwash*;

'Launching from the ship, the A-3B frequently tanks returning strike aircraft, flies its bombing mission and, before landing, refuels the next group of strike aircraft. In addition, the A-3B is the "Grey Line" vehicle for sightseers from correspondents to visiting statesmen to the Captain of the ship. When the bomb-bay is not loaded with bombs the A-3B provides a jet COD [carrier onboard delivery] service, delivering mail, aircraft parts and other high priority items.'

Another VAH-4 group, Det Mike, which called themselves the 'Red Barons', reported 108,000 lbs of bombs dropped from USS *Enterprise* (CVAN-65) that same year while also passing 1.7 million pounds of fuel to other aircraft. The 'Whale' continued to be used as a bomber through to the end of 1967, and it appears to have wrapped up ordnance delivery by mid-1968. The aircraft's criticality as a tanker, its vulnerability and the availability of other, more capable strikers had eventually led to its removal from the ordnance-delivery role. In one of the community's lingering tales, Gen William Westmoreland, the senior US commander in-theatre, reportedly himself ordered the end of Skywarrior bombing when, on a visit to a carrier, he was aghast to find out that A-3Bs were providing close air support to 'his' Army troops without the benefit of a proper bombsight. Even if this is possibly not quite 'true', it certainly makes for a colourful story!

PASSING GAS

Late-build A-3Bs had been delivered from Douglas with the ability to have a hose-drum unit installed in the bomb-bay to carry out aerial refuelling. This capability was eventually extended to all B-models. By 1965 every jet in the air wing had a refuelling probe installed, and by then the 'Whale' was the primary tanker – 'buddy store' equipped attack aircraft frequently 'passed gas' as well.

Among the early duties performed by the tanker 'Whales' was to act as pathfinders for A-4s on possible nuclear strike missions. Without the auxiliary bomb-bay fuel tank the aircraft could carry a nuclear weapon itself, and would, as the plan went, still be able to fuel the 'Scooters' and provide navigation support before they headed off for their separate targets. Needless to say, it was a grim mission that few pilots seriously thought they would return from.

By 1967 practically all A-3Bs carried the refuelling package as a semi-permanent fixture. Most aircraft also carried a long optional auxiliary bomb-bay fuel tank that held an additional 4400 lbs of fuel in place of weapons. Finally, in May of that year, tanker-equipped A-3Bs were re-designated KA-3Bs, with at least 66 bombers being given this designation by September.

With the auxiliary bomb-bay tank installed, the KA-3 had the greatest amount of fuel 'give' of any of the US Navy's carrier-based tankers, with either 35,000 lbs of JP-5 available for off-load or in excess of 20,000 lbs during a normal one-and-a-half hour launch and recovery cycle. Other, buddy-store equipped, aircraft augmented the 'Whales', but offered considerably less fuel – the A-4C could pass 9800 lbs and the A-7 about 13,000 lbs. Even the later KA-6D, which also had an internally mounted hose-drum unit, had 'only' about 23,500 lbs of fuel to contribute off the catapult (all numbers are for JP-5, which weighed 6.8 lbs per gallon).

Customers included all US Navy and US Marine Corps aircraft, as well as those USAF types still using the hose-and-drogue method of refuelling, including the F-100, F-104, F-105 (which also had a boom receptacle),

'Push-back on the "Whale", Cat 2!' The pilot of a VAH-10 Det 62 KA-3B has taxied a little bit too far forward and needs the help of the flightdeck crew to be pushed back into position. Events like this could drive the Air Boss crazy, as it needlessly delayed a launch cycle and was fraught with peril as both engines would be turning and highly susceptible to FOD. This shot is from 'Indy's' 1968 Mediterranean deployment with CVW-7 (*US Navy*)

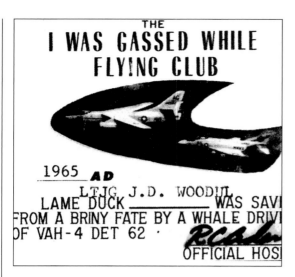

THE
I WAS GASSED WHILE
FLYING CLUB

1965 AD
LTJG J.D. WOODUL
LAME DUCK _____ WAS SAV[ED]
FROM A BRINY FATE BY A WHALE DRIV[ER]
OF VAH-4 DET 62 · *RCA[...]*

OFFICIAL HOS[...]

VAH-4 Det 62 presented these cards to CVW-7 aircrew who were saved by timely A-3 tanking during the air wing's 1965 deployment on board CVA-62. This one was given to Lt(jg) Jack Woodul, an A-4E pilot with VA-86 (*via Jack Woodul*)

The primary 'Whale' mission during the Vietnam War – tanking. Here, a VAH-4 Det C A-3B refuels a VF-213 F-4B during CVA-63's 1966-67 cruise (*US Navy via Rich Dann*)

RF-101 and B-66. The 'Whale's' refuelling package was described by one veteran fighter pilot as the 'Gold Standard' for hose-and-drogue tankers, being more stable and reliable than any other tanker he had ever worked with. In fact the KA-3 was overwhelmingly preferred to even the USAF KC-135, whose notoriously unforgiving, hard basket was derisively referred to as 'The Iron Maiden' by US Navy crews.

Dealing with the USAF was not always amicable as some leaders from both services officially discouraged 'sharing' fuel in the belief that it would help boost sortie counts for the other service, as if the air war was some odd competition.

It is not exaggerating to say that A-3 crews 'wrote the book' on how to tank around the boat, with the 'Whale' proving equally adept in both overhead and mission roles. The KA-3 was frequently the first aircraft off the flightdeck at the start of the launch cycle, quickly climbing to 6000-7000 ft to top off with whatever the off-going tanker had left. They would then switch positions, with the off-going aircraft checking the refuelling package of the new tanker before it descended into the landing pattern for recovery.

Overhead tanking would usually start directly above the carrier, with freshly launched fighter and attack aircraft rendezvousing and taking 2000-3000 lbs of fuel before proceeding on their assigned tasks. When operating as a mission tanker, the KA-3 would press well ahead of the launch and be available to refuel jets just prior to them going 'feet dry'. The 'Whale's' high speed meant that it usually had little trouble getting into position ahead of the strike. The tanker would then loiter off the beach, listening to the strike frequency to identify who would need fuel on the way back to the carrier.

Post-strike work could also include 'wet-wing' tanking, where A-3s met damaged aircraft right off the beach and refuelled them all the way to the ship, with fuel at times pouring out of the receiver almost as quickly as the 'Whale' passed it. This procedure – particularly effective with A-4

Skyhawks thanks to their wing design – saved multiple aircraft during the war. Most 'Whale' detachments kept a scoreboard of the number of aircraft they saved during deployment, and made sure that the rest of the air wing knew their value.

Recovery KA-3s typically hung out over the carrier at 6000 ft in the 'tanker circle', watching how things progressed in case their services were needed. Listening to the tower frequency, crews knew which jets were having problems or were low on fuel, and they put their aircraft where they could do the most good accordingly. Pilots 'hawked' the pattern and would descend to follow an aircraft calling 'trick or treat', where he either trapped, tanked or 'bingo'ed' to the nearest land divert airfield. Good KA-3 pilots would time their run in over the carrier to be at 1200 ft just off the ship's starboard bow when the aircraft in question was over the ramp. If he trapped, they would climb back up into the tanker circle. If the customer 'boltered' (missed a wire) or was waved off, the pilot only needed to look up at his 'two o'clock' to see the KA-3 with its basket coming out, ready to plug. Needless to say, it was a welcome sight to many pilots 'sweating' low fuel states.

Even with the significant amount of fuel the A-3 had to give, one of the type's peculiarities meant that the jet itself could only carry a relatively small amount of fuel to allow it to safely land back onboard a carrier. With a 'max trap' weight of 49,000 lbs, the average 'Whale' would have no more than 5000 lbs of fuel onboard to recover with – typically good for only two or three passes, depending on weather and how far away the divert airfield was. Since the tanker was usually the last aircraft to recover at the end of a cycle, it meant that KA-3 pilots had to get aboard with limited options available. Most did it with aplomb.

Demand for the 'Whale's' services remained high as the war progressed. In January 1966 VAH-4 deployed Det Yankee to NAS Cubi Point, in the Philippines, for more than five months, the land-based detachment fulfilling a variety of requirements for Seventh Fleet. Det OinC was the

The WestPac sailor's home away from home was Cubi Point, in the Philippines. The base, located on Subic Bay, provided both a safe harbour and a pier for carriers. Located about 720 nautical miles from Da Nang, it proved to be an absolutely critical supply and maintenance facility for operations over North Vietnam. It also had the legendary liberty town of Olongapo to tend to the fleet's other 'needs'. This view, apparently taken just prior to the war, shows two VAH-4 detachments sharing the Cubi ramp with a US Marine Corps UH-34 squadron (*via Rich Dann*)

In the A-3 community Jet Assisted Take-Off (JATO) was intended to get nuclear strike aircraft airborne from damaged runways or carriers. It would be routinely used in Southeast Asia, however, to get heavy aircraft off the ground in hot and humid conditions at places like Cubi Point. Here, a VAH-4 A3D-2 dramatically demonstrates the technique circa 1960 (*US Navy*)

A VAH-4 Det 63 KA-3B takes the No 3 wire on *Kitty Hawk* during the 1967-68 deployment, with aircraft from VF-213 and RVAH-11 looking on. Heavy Four was an early proponent of the use of tanker stripes to help receivers locate the correct tanker in a gaggle. In most (but not all) cases the number of stripes equalled the last digit of the nose Modex number, the limit being six (*US Navy via Tailhook Association*)

remarkable Lt Cdr Bill Barnes, fresh from his tour with VAH-8. 'The det had two aircraft, ZB 000 and ZB 001, and we were *fantastic*', he stated, 'and we were welcomed on every flightdeck in the Gulf of Tonkin because we brought mail and fresh food out to them. Our troops were great, and they worked hard to keep our aircraft up, but then they also had liberty every night in Olongapo to look forward to!'

Det Yankee, also known as the 'Hollygreen Giants', worked out of Da Nang, in South Vietnam, as well. According to Barnes, they also carried out bombing sorties, with ordnance delivered in places including Mu Gia Pass, on the Ho Chi Minh Trail. Departures from Cubi frequently required use of JATO due to heavy weights and steamy tropical conditions – 'at one point we ran Cubi out of JATO bottles', Barnes remembered. The 'Giants' flew in excess of 500 sorties with their two aircraft and passed more than 1.2 million pounds of fuel during their deployment, before returning to Whidbey Island.

As for Lt Cdr Barnes, he moved on to VAH-10 and took Det 66 out as OinC for a Mediterranean cruise in 1967 embarked in USS *America* (CVA-66). During the deployment he would launch with live weapons as part of the immediate response to the Israeli attack on USS *Liberty* (AGTR-4) on 8 June. The resulting strike package ('very disorganised, with no targets assigned at launch', according to Barnes) rendezvoused, awaited instructions and was subsequently ordered to return to the ship. He would eventually transfer to the RA-5C community.

With *Midway* entering the yards for heavy work VAH-8 transferred to CVW-15, where it deployed with five aircraft in *Constellation* in May 1966. A third war deployment, again in 'Connie' but now as a member of CVW-14, started in May 1967, still as a complete squadron *(text continues on page 45)*.

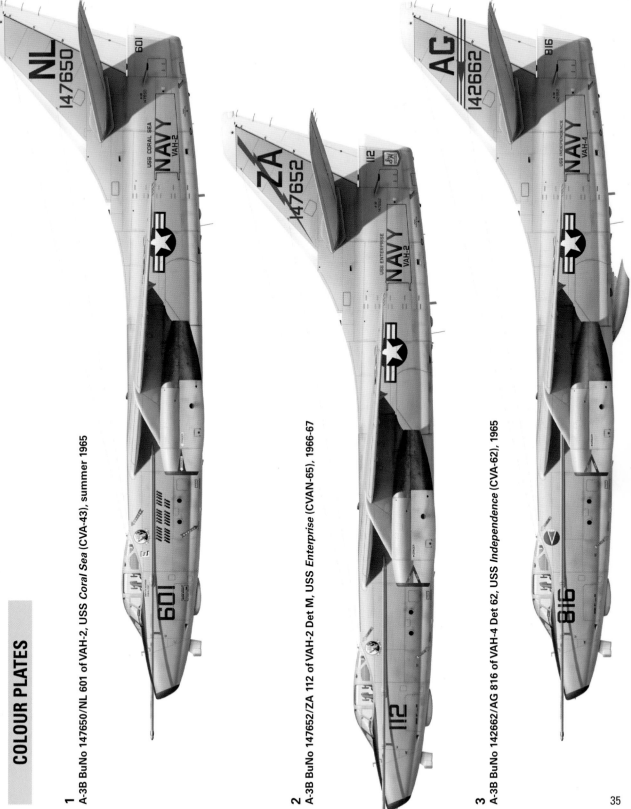

1
A-3B BuNo 147650/NL 601 of VAH-2, USS *Coral Sea* (CVA-43), summer 1965

2
A-3B BuNo 147652/ZA 112 of VAH-2 Det M, USS *Enterprise* (CVAN-65), 1966-67

3
A-3B BuNo 142662/AG 816 of VAH-4 Det 62, USS *Independence* (CVA-62), 1965

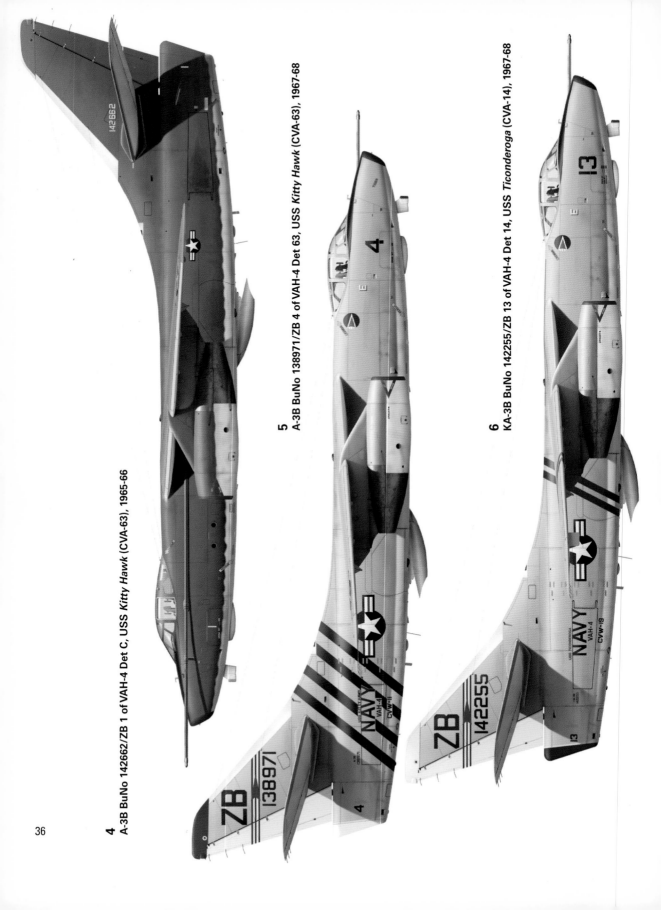

4
A-3B BuNo 142662/ZB 1 of VAH-4 Det C, USS *Kitty Hawk* (CVA-63), 1965-66

5
A-3B BuNo 138971/ZB 4 of VAH-4 Det 63, USS *Kitty Hawk* (CVA-63), 1967-68

6
KA-3B BuNo 142255/ZB 13 of VAH-4 Det 14, USS *Ticonderoga* (CVA-14), 1967-68

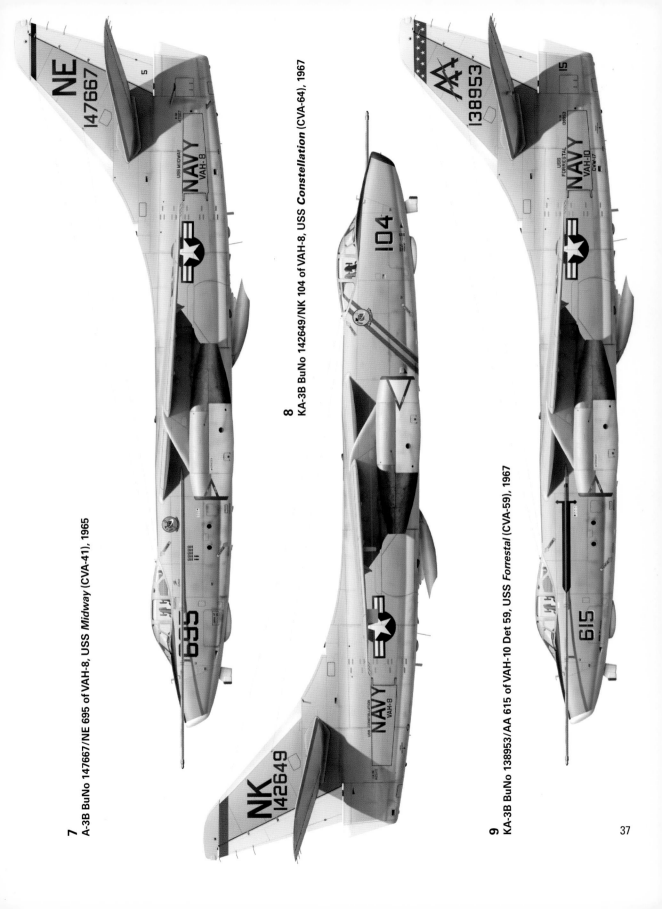

7
A-3B BuNo 147667/NE 695 of VAH-8, USS *Midway* (CVA-41), 1965

8
KA-3B BuNo 142649/NK 104 of VAH-8, USS *Constellation* (CVA-64), 1967

9
KA-3B BuNo 138953/AA 615 of VAH-10 Det 59, USS *Forrestal* (CVA-59), 1967

37

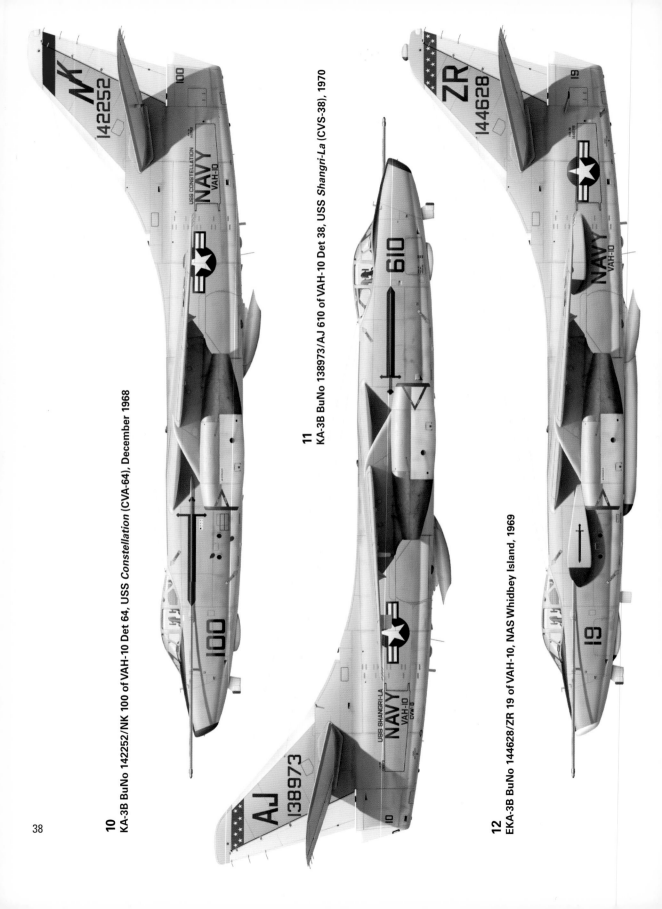

10
KA-3B BuNo 142252/NK 100 of VAH-10 Det 64, USS *Constellation* (CVA-64), December 1968

11
KA-3B BuNo 138973/AJ 610 of VAH-10 Det 38, USS *Shangri-La* (CVS-38), 1970

12
EKA-3B BuNo 144628/ZR 19 of VAH-10, NAS Whidbey Island, 1969

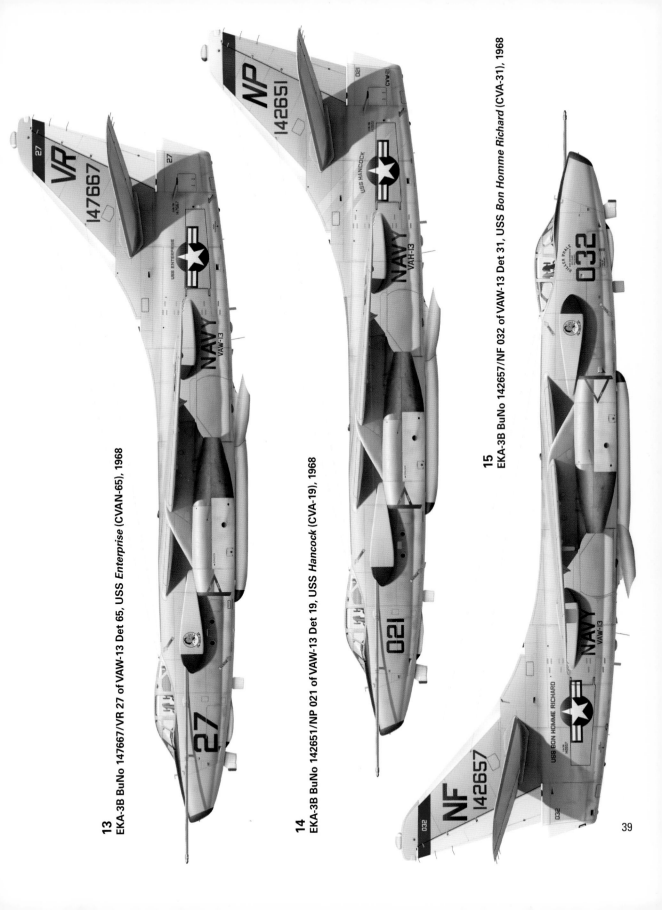

13
EKA-3B BuNo 147667/VR 27 of VAW-13 Det 65, USS *Enterprise* (CVAN-65), 1968

14
EKA-3B BuNo 142651/NP 021 of VAW-13 Det 19, USS *Hancock* (CVA-19), 1968

15
EKA-3B BuNo 142657/NF 032 of VAW-13 Det 31, USS *Bon Homme Richard* (CVA-31), 1968

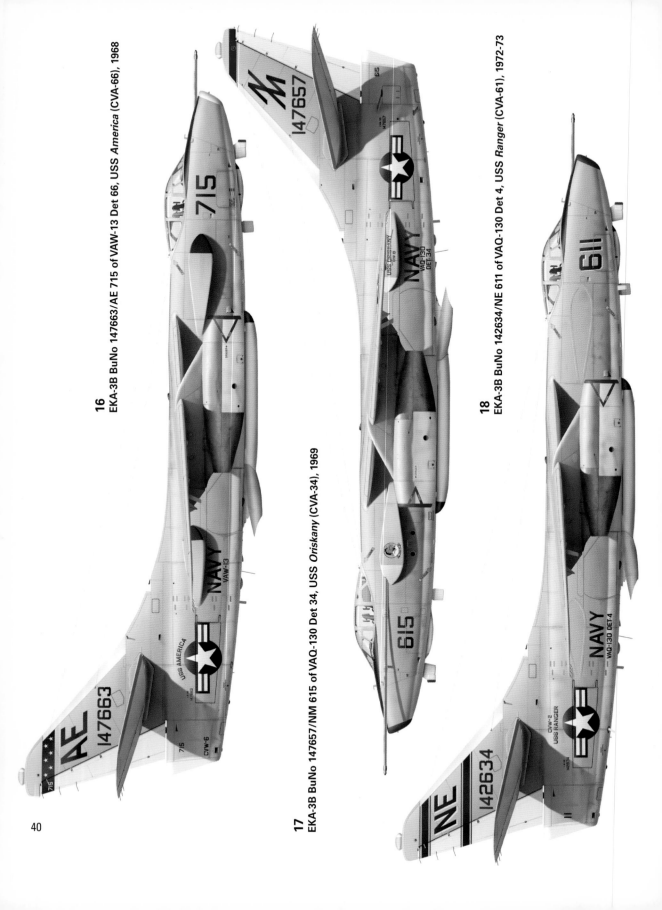

16
EKA-3B BuNo 147663/AE 715 of VAW-13 Det 66, USS *America* (CVA-66), 1968

17
EKA-3B BuNo 147657/NM 615 of VAQ-130 Det 34, USS *Oriskany* (CVA-34), 1969

18
EKA-3B BuNo 142634/NE 611 of VAQ-130 Det 4, USS *Ranger* (CVA-61), 1972-73

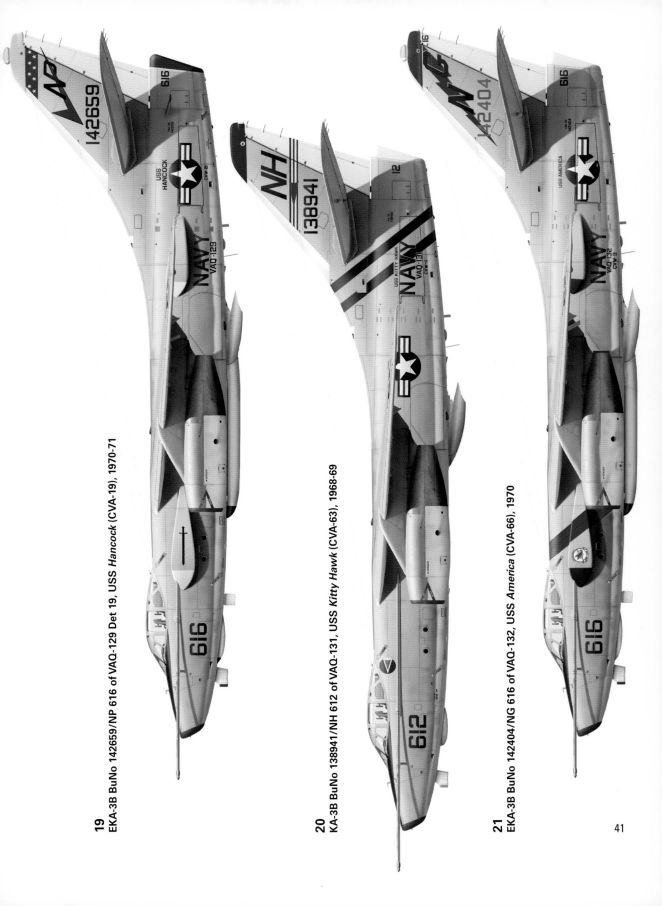

19
EKA-3B BuNo 142659/NP 616 of VAQ-129 Det 19, USS *Hancock* (CVA-19), 1970-71

20
KA-3B BuNo 138941/NH 612 of VAQ-131, USS *Kitty Hawk* (CVA-63), 1968-69

21
EKA-3B BuNo 142404/NG 616 of VAQ-132, USS *America* (CVA-66), 1970

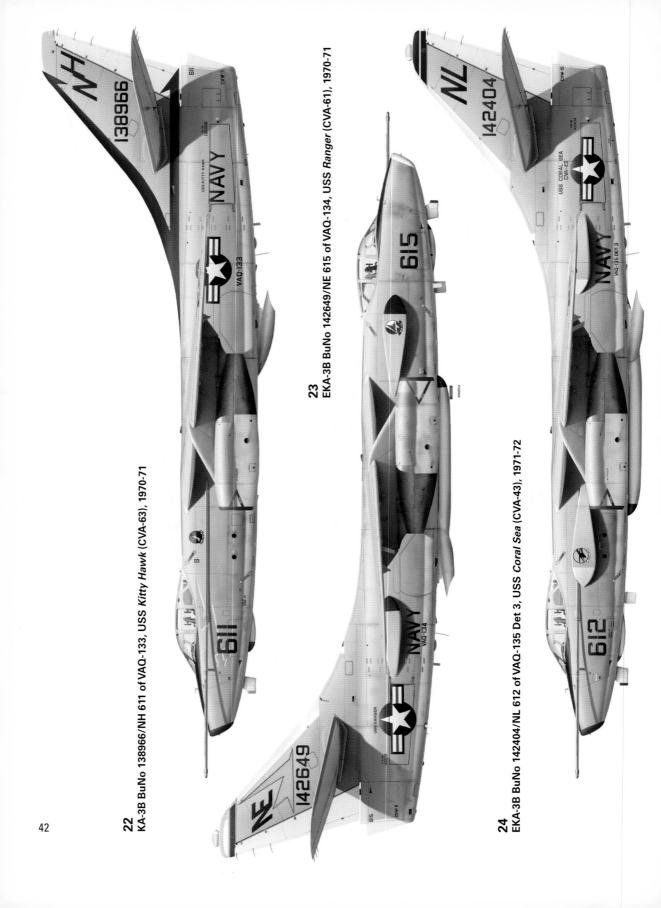

22
KA-3B BuNo 138966/NH 611 of VAQ-133, USS *Kitty Hawk* (CVA-63), 1970-71

23
EKA-3B BuNo 142649/NE 615 of VAQ-134, USS *Ranger* (CVA-61), 1970-71

24
EKA-3B BuNo 142404/NL 612 of VAQ-135 Det 3, USS *Coral Sea* (CVA-43), 1971-72

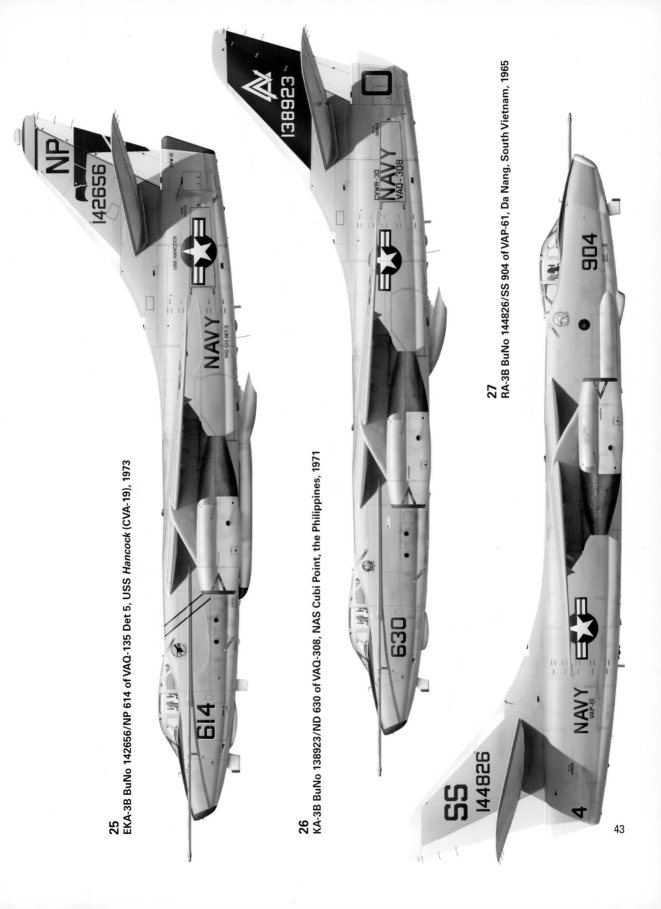

25
EKA-3B BuNo 142656/NP 614 of VAQ-135 Det 5, USS *Hancock* (CVA-19), 1973

26
KA-3B BuNo 138923/ND 630 of VAQ-308, NAS Cubi Point, the Philippines, 1971

27
RA-3B BuNo 144826/SS 904 of VAP-61, Da Nang, South Vietnam, 1965

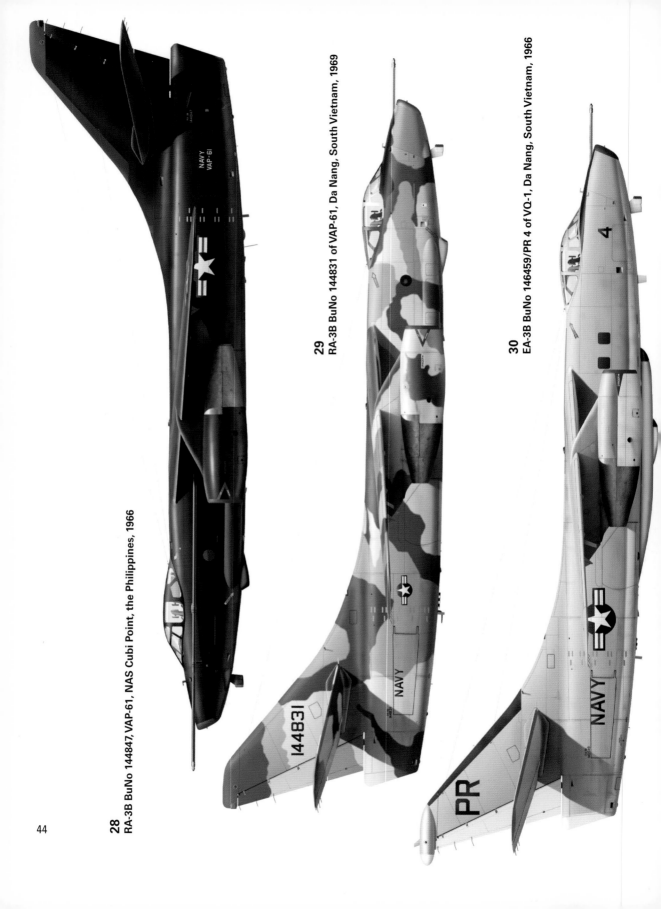

28
RA-3B BuNo 144847, VAP-61, NAS Cubi Point, the Philippines, 1966

29
RA-3B BuNo 144831 of VAP-61, Da Nang, South Vietnam, 1969

30
EA-3B BuNo 146459/PR 4 of VQ-1, Da Nang, South Vietnam, 1966

While VAH-2, -4 and -8 were busy sending aircraft to combat in Vietnam, VAH-10 had quietly become the preferred unit for Atlantic Fleet deployments. The 'Vikings' had conducted two cruisers in *Constellation* to WestPac, the second of which, in 1964-65, marking the last time 12 A-3Bs would be sent to sea as one squadron. With the rapid transition of the Sanford Skywarrior community to Vigilantes, the US Navy still needed to send A-3s to Sixth Fleet for tanking duties. VAH-10 got the job, and in May 1965 the squadron embarked six aircraft in USS *Franklin D Roosevelt* (CVA-42) for a cruise to the Mediterranean as part of CVW-1.

Through to late 1968, VAH-10 would support only AirLant carriers, which inevitably became involved in combat in Vietnam when they too were sent to war. Det 42 deployed four KA-3Bs with *Roosevelt* to the Western Pacific in June 1966. In June 1967 Det 59 reported aboard *Forrestal* for the first cruise ever by CVW-17. It would be involved in the tragic ship fire of 29 July that abruptly halted the deployment. The next VAH-10 det to Vietnam would be aboard *America* in 1968, with two KA-3Bs being mixed with an EKA-3B det from VAW-13.

LOSSES

Twenty A-3s of all varieties were lost worldwide between 8 February 1965 and 3 November 1967. Two were bombers in combat situations. On 12 April 1966 a VAH-4 Det C A-3B was shot down by Chinese J-6s (MiG-19s) with 30 mm gunfire. The aircraft (BuNo 142653/ZB 3) was flying from Cubi Point to *Kitty Hawk* when it was intercepted, the Chinese government stating that it had been destroyed over the Luichow Peninsula, just north of Hainan Island. All four of the men onboard, Lt Cdr Bill Glasson, Lt(jg) Larry Jordan, PR2 Ken Pugh and ATR2 Reuben Harris, were killed. The Chinese had also reported shooting down an RA-3B on 5 October 1965, although US Navy records do not corroborate this claim.

Kitty Hawk conducts Underway Replenishment (UNREP) during its first war cruise, in 1965-66, with the USS *Mazama* (AE-9) and destroyer USS *Agerholm* (DD-826) alongside. Some 46 CVW-11 aircraft are visible, of 78 assigned. Notable are the number of camouflaged aircraft present as part of the air wing's unsuccessful experiment with camouflage paint during the deployment. There are four 'Whales' on deck – a single VQ-1 EA-3B sits between elevators one and two, and three of VAH-4 Det C's A-3Bs can also be seen, including ZB 1 in green paint spotted on the starboard quarter aft of the E-2s (*US Navy via Tailhook Association*)

Lt Cdr Tom Maxwell (right) shakes hands with VAH-4 Det G/34 OinC Bill Laurentis during the 1968 cruise in *Oriskany*. Laurentis wears a torso harness with survival gear attached, including a 0.38-cal special revolver at his hip. Maxwell's detachment cap has four footprints on the peak in a wry reference to the squadron's 'Four-Runner' nickname (*US Navy via Tom Maxwell*)

Almost a year later, and on its next deployment, VAH-4 Det C lost another aircraft on 8 March 1967 when BuNo 144627/ZB 5 failed to return to the 'Hawk' after a night mining mission along the Kien Giang River near Dong Hoi. It was presumed that the aircraft was either shot down or had flown into the water. Lt Cdr Carroll Crain, Lt(jg) George Pawlish and ATN2 Ron Galvin were all listed as killed in action.

While the aircraft had a reputation for being challenging to land, it was during catapult shots that the type suffered most of its losses in-theatre – typically from failure of the bridle itself. VAH-4 Det G was launching BuNo 138947/ZB 10 on 25 May from *Oriskany* when it suffered such a failure on the cat shot. The aeroplane went into the water off the bow, and although all four men aboard were safely recovered, the pilot, Det OinC Lt Cdr Richard Walls and B/N Lt(jg) Jerry Adams both suffered fractured legs as the cockpit broke apart on impact. Walls would eventually return to flight duty, only to be killed in June 1970 as XO of VA-145 when the wing of his Intruder failed while dive-bombing at Boardman, Oregon.

Another VAH-4 jet was lost on launch from *Enterprise* on April Fools' Day 1966 when Det Mike's BuNo 142665/ZB 112 appeared to suffer a nose gear failure at the cat shot. The aircraft failed to gain flight speed and impacted the water. B/N Lt(jg) Bill Kohlrusch was recovered by the plane guard helo, but subsequently died onboard ship. Cdr Bill Grayson and ADJ1 Melvin Krech were lost with the aircraft.

On 2 October 1966 *Coral Sea* was launching aircraft into Cubi Point at the end of a line period when VAH-2 Det A had an aircraft suffer either a bridle or cat hook failure that resulted in the jet (BuNo 142633) going over the side. The pilot, Lt Charlie Celler, and his three crewmen all survived. Thirteen months later, on 3 November 1967, VAH-8 had an aircraft (BuNo 147653) crash off *Constellation* following a cat shot off the waist – all three onboard, Lt Cdr Pete Krusi, Lt(jg) Hans Grauert and ADJ2 Richard Sandifer, were killed. Failure of the bridle was listed as the probable cause of the crash.

ORISKANY AND VAH-4 DET GOLF

Tom Maxwell was a USAF brat who graduated from Kemper Military Academy at Boonville, Missouri, in 1955. He subsequently went through the NAVCAD programme and earned his Wings of Gold in April 1957, before heading to Utility Squadron One at Barber's Point, Hawaii, where he flew Grumman Hellcats and Douglas JD-1 Invaders. Fleet duty followed as an S2F Tracker pilot with VS-37 aboard USS *Hornet* (CVS-12). After a staff tour with NORAD at Colorado Springs, Maxwell was ordered to VAH-123 for training in A-3s. He eventually joined the 'Four-Runners' of VAH-4, and would make two very eventful cruises with Det Golf in *Oriskany* as a member of CVW-16;

'We dropped some bombs on the first cruise but none at all on the second, where we did about 80 percent tanking and 20 percent as "Fast CODs", moving supplies – particularly mail and people from Cubi to the ship.

'We'd typically launch as a tanker as the first aircraft off the bow, pass more than 20,000 lbs of gas to outgoing strikers and then recover for hot-fuelling, which led to another cat shot as the recovery tanker. We could get up to three flights a day in this fashion.

'Working the Gulf, you had to be very aware of where Hainan Island was. We were supposed to stay at least 20 miles away from it as the Chinese were very aggressive with their MiGs if you got too close. Likewise, during 1967 Seventh Fleet had ordered tankers to never go over North Vietnam due to their vulnerability, so we pretty much stayed over the water.'

CVW-16 lost 25 aircraft on the 1966 deployment, but no 'Whales'. There were successes as well, as VF-162's CO, the irrepressible Cdr Dick 'Belly' Bellinger shot down a MiG-21 on 9 October. Maxwell got the job of taking Bellinger to Saigon for a press briefing after the event;

The joy of being home. Lt Cdr Tom Maxwell is reunited with his family at Whidbey Island at the end of the 1966 *Oriskany* deployment in mid-November. This event was particularly emotional coming after the ship's tragic fire. With Tom are his son, Matthew Thomas Maxwell IV, daughter Debra Ann and his wife Betty Ann (*US Navy via Tom Maxwell*)

'Dick had been given access to the Doc's "medicinal alcohol" onboard, and he was in a *very* good mood as we flew towards Saigon. He wanted to fly the aircraft, but I figured that wasn't a really good idea. I did manage a perfect "tuck under" break (a 270-degree roll to enter the pattern) at Ton Son Nhut though. That got peoples' attention, and I certainly heard about it after landing.'

The first deployment ended in the massive ship fire of 26 October 1966. Maxwell had drawn what he thought was a bad deal by getting the first tanker launch of the day while the rest of CVW-16 was still asleep. He was on the flightdeck aft when the fire alarms sounded. The fire was caused by a mishandled magnesium flare setting off an entire locker full of the devices. The resulting conflagration swept through the forward part of the ship, killing 44. Among the dead were Det OinC Lt Cdr George Farris and his roommate, Jim Smith, both of whom died in their stateroom. Maxwell took over as acting OinC until relieved by Lt Cdr Bill Laurentis, who relieved him at Cubi. Both men remained with the unit during its short seven-month turnaround for its next deployment.

Oriskany was quickly repaired and left Alameda on 16 June 1967 for the war zone on a cruise where it would lose more aircraft than any other carrier during the war – 39 lost to all causes over the seven-month deployment. As was typical of many 'Whale' detachments, Det Golf did not accompany the ship across the Pacific but flew ahead in order to get into theatre early. The detachment launched its first combat tanker sortie from Cubi Point on 29 June, two weeks before *Oriskany* started its first line period. Det Golf's primary role remained tanking, with three KA-3Bs

VF-111's Lt Cdr Dick Schaffert strikes a pose beside a 'Sundowner' F-8C aboard *Oriskany* in 1967-68. He had been saved by the direct intervention of Lt Cdr Tom Maxwell and his crew onboard VAH-4 Det G's duty KA-3B on 18 July 1967 when they chose to ignore standing orders and fly their jet inland over enemy territory to rendezvous with Schaffert's fuel-starved Crusader (*Dick Schaffert via Peter Mersky*)

assigned. The first line period started on 14 July, and within three days CVW-16 had lost four aircraft – two A-4Es, an A-1H and an F-8E – with three of the four pilots being recovered. Things only got worse on the 18th.

Maxwell had been scheduled for a morning tanker hop off the 'O-Boat' in AH 611 (BuNo 142655). Needless to say, the ship and air wing were busy – the day prior he had flown three flights in AH 610, logging 7.1 hours of 'green ink' (combat time). The CVW-16 aircraft had run into heavy opposition on a morning strike, with a VA-164 A-4E (BuNo 151986/AH 404) being shot down at 0913 hrs by 37 mm AAA about 65 miles inland near the targets – bridges at Phu Ly. Lt Cdr Dick Hartman was down and a Combat Search and Rescue (C-SAR) effort was initiated to recover him.

Lt Cdr Dick 'Brown Bear' Schaffert, flying VF-111 F-8C 'Old Nick 101' (BuNo 146991) came off his BARCAP over the water to help provide cover. He was headed towards Hartman's reported position when he realised there was another Skyhawk down. The jet (BuNo 151175/AH 415) flown by Lt(jg) Larry Duthie had also been hit by 37 mm rounds while over Hartman, forcing the pilot to eject before he had made it to the coast. As 'Brown Bear' had discovered, Duthie had come down near Nam Dinh. There were now two active rescues going on, separated by about 12 miles. Schaffert took the on-scene commander role over Duthie and remained in the area, calling in support while dodging SA-2s and a considerable amount of AAA – all this while watching his fuel gauge drop.

Meanwhile, Maxwell and his crew had recovered onboard *Oriskany* at the end of their first sortie. They were directed to remain in the aircraft and 'hot pump' (refuel with engines turning) in preparation for immediate launch. The squadron intelligence officer came up the hatch and told them about the rapidly evolving SAR effort for the pair of Skyhawk pilots. Refuelling complete, they launched and took up a tanker position about 20 miles off the coast, while following efforts on the SAR radio frequency as helicopters and more aircraft were brought in.

With additional A-4s inbound to take the overhead SAR effort, Schaffert finally turned his Crusader's nose to the east, fully realising he might not have enough fuel to make the Gulf, let alone the boat. In their KA-3B, Maxwell and his crew had heard Schaffert's Mayday call. 'I looked around my cockpit and immediately received two emphatic "thumbs up" from the other men – Lt(jg) Jim Vanderhoek and ADJ1 Bill Shelton. There was no discussion about what we had to do at that point'. He immediately pushed the 'Whale's' throttles up and turned for the beach.

'We knew we were now violating standing Seventh Fleet orders that no A-3 would go feet dry, yet we also knew that if this Crusader didn't get fuel they'd have another man down in North Vietnam.'

With the help of the *Red Crown* (the code name for the Positive Identification Radar Advisory Zone controller who provided US aircraft with radar coverage of North Vietnam via ship-mounted air search radar)

A lovely pod of 'Whales' – VAH-4 Det G/34 returns to Whidbey Island at the end of the 1967-68 *Oriskany* cruise with their three KA-3Bs, along with ZB 6 that was sent up by the squadron to meet the incoming jets. The det had completed a transpacific crossing ahead of the ship, returning ZB 610, ZB 611 and ZB 612 (two of these jets were replacements for aircraft lost on deployment) (*US Navy via Tom Maxwell*)

ship, Maxwell flew his aircraft between 30 and 40 miles inland and started a hard right turn in front of Schaffert's F-8, while his B/N extended the refuelling hose. While all of this was taking place, random flak bursts were going off nearby, and the crew's radar warning gear blared in their ears, indicating SAM activity in the area.

Schaffert saw the 'Whale' turning in front of him and had his refuelling probe out as he made a hot approach for the basket. He plugged on the first try and looked down to see the fuel needle moving away from 'empty' as JP-5 started replacing air in his Crusader's tanks. The pair stayed plugged in almost all the way to the coast, the F-8 taking more than 1200 lbs of fuel on the way. *Oriskany* had a ready deck for them on arrival, and they both trapped successfully. The 'Whale' crew logged 3.1 hours of combat time for the morning's work.

The saving of Dick Schaffert and his jet by Tom Maxwell and his VAH-4 crew were the only positive aspects of an otherwise grim day for CVW-16. Adding to the tragedy was the loss of a 'Big Mother' SH-3A with four crewmen whilst trying to recover Hartman on the 19th. Another A-4E would also be lost during the effort when Lt(jg) Barry Wood's aircraft (BuNo 152034/AH 401) was hit by AAA and he was forced to eject over the water, being recovered. Hartman himself was subsequently captured and died in captivity. Duthie was eventually rescued by a USAF HH-3E Jolly Green Giant.

Ironically, Maxwell and his crew received no official recognition for their flight, since they had violated a Seventh Fleet order. They did receive the undying admiration of the other members of CVW-16, however, for their bravery and flying skills in the A-3.

Among the 39 aircraft lost by CVW-16 during its 1967 deployment were two of Det Golf's jets. On 28 July 1967 KA-3B BuNo 142658 (which had only been converted into a tanker by the Naval Air Rework Facility (NARF) at Alameda the previous month) was attempting to fly over a massive thunderstorm in the Gulf of Tonkin when both engines flamed out. The pilot, Lt Cdr Mike Kavenaugh, ordered the crew to bail out. While he was rescued, the B/N, Ens Bruce Patterson and crewman AE2 Charles Hardie, were not recovered.

The 21 October 1967 crash of BuNo 142655 destroyed the aircraft that Tom Maxwell had used on his 18 July mission, 'Holly Green 611' taking off from Cubi on a tanking mission at maximum weight and in temperature conditions that required use of JATO at the time. With normal acceleration, the pilot, Lt Cdr Don Albright, fired the rockets after 3000 ft of roll, only to have one bottle on the right side break free upon ignition. It caromed off the starboard main mount, which duly separated from the aircraft. The device then deflected into the No 2 engine and sheared the fuel control, causing it to fail while the aircraft was only 100 ft above the runway.

The pilot called a quick 'Mayday' as the 'Whale' just missed the duty fire truck by the side of the runway and lurched towards the water in the general direction of Grande Island. The aircraft hit the bay almost wings level due to what was later described as Albright's superb airmanship in an impossible circumstance. All four men onboard (Albright, B/N Lt(jg) Jim Skinner, enlisted crewman Lindsay and PN2 Ralph Estes) managed to clear the wreck and were recovered, with injuries that ran from broken vertebrae to simple fractures.

Det G (now officially designated Det 34) ended its deployment as it had begun, taking the surviving KA-3Bs across the Pacific ahead of the ship. The jets arrived home at Whidbey on 27 January 1968, finishing up a roughly seven-month cruise during which Maxwell had made 152 flights totalling 332 hours. He had also logged 144 arrested landings.

Tom Maxwell would subsequently fly with VQ-2 in Rota and make another trip to Vietnam in EA-3Bs. Later made CO of VAQ-135 and overseeing its move to Whidbey Island for EA-6B transition in 1973, he eventually retired as a captain. Maxwell currently lives in Missouri and is heavily involved with the Prison Fellowship Ministries organisation established by former Watergate participant Charles Colson.

'WHALE' TALES

The mystique of the 'Whale' was undeniable, and to many it still retains the fleet 'record' for being 'the largest aircraft to ever operate off an aircraft carrier'. That description is not quite correct however. Granted, decades later, the Skywarrior still holds the record as having taken the heaviest catapult shot ever from a ship (tested up to 84,000 lbs from *Saratoga* in 1959), the F-14D Tomcat could land heavier and the E-2 Hawkeye, with an 80 ft wingspan, has wider dimensions. And this completely ignores the limited carrier operations of the C-130 and U-2.

The real point was that the A-3 did it as a tactical jet off of the fabled '27C' modified *Essex* class carriers, and their crews did it 'without a net' – i.e., no ejection seats.

In spite of the sober image befitting the size of their aircraft and seriousness of their mission, A-3 crews occasionally showed themselves to be as wild as their fighter and attack brethren in the air wing, and their occasional antics with the big aircraft became the stuff of legend. These tales, some of which defy belief, remain solidly in the category of 'sea stories', with the veracity of the event having to be balanced by the enthusiasm, and relative sobriety, of the person telling it. They include verified stories of flights under both the Golden Gate and Bay Bridges near Alameda. More amazing is the report of at least one 'Whale' flying

under Deception Pass Bridge – the high steel-arch structure that connects Whidbey and Fidalgo Islands in Washington State.

One 'Zapper' pilot, with the somewhat disquieting call-sign 'Crash', was renowned for taking a bet at the NAS Fallon bar and conducting a touch-and-go between vehicle traffic on Interstate Highway 80 in broad daylight. On arrival the Nevada State Police reportedly found two strips of rubber spanning 10 ft 5 in, which was, coincidentally, the exact distance between the main gear legs of the A-3. The same operator was also known for taking girlfriends on unauthorised flights – something his OinC reportedly discovered at Cubi Point when he saw a pair of shapely legs in a skirt come out of the boarding hatch at the end of a flight from Clark AFB. The woman turned out to be an American teacher that 'Crash' had met at the USAF bar the night before. The lieutenant was soon in hack (restricted to quarters), and the det found an alternate route for his lady friend back to her starting point.

VAW-13 was famed for maintaining the 'Zapper Lounge' at the Cubi Bachelor Officer's Quarters (BOQ), where aviators knew they could always find a cold drink and comradeship at any time of the day or night. The lounge was a holdover from the squadron's EA-1F days, and it was maintained by the unit's junior officer, or 'Baby Zapper' – one of whom (Skyraider Naval Aviation Observer Grady Jackson) would eventually reach the rank of rear admiral.

Perhaps the standout 'Whale Tale' is the legend of the 'Golden Goddess', known community-wide as 'GG' or 'Gigi'. The latter was a 43-inch statuette of a naked woman that had been 'liberated' in 1958 from the lobby of Tim's Restaurant, a popular watering hole located on Webster Street in Alameda. CPO Cliff Hornung from VAH-4 Det Delta literally walked out with the statue one night and took her to *Hancock*, aboard which she made her first deployment. The rest of the Whidbey A3D community took notice, and she immediately became the object of intense desire that led to years of increasingly sophisticated raids to claim her.

'Gigi' survived through to the very end of A-3s at Whidbey and eventually moved to Alameda with the new VAQ community. In the early 1970s she returned to Whidbey, where the new EA-6B squadrons continued the tradition. According to one version, the 'Golden Goddess', damaged from years of abuse, was given a burial at sea by VAQ-131 in the early 1980s apparently by a group of junior officers who were actually tired of dealing with her.

In a community full of colourful characters, one that stood out was Cdr John Wunsch. Noted for his fiery red handlebar moustache, Wunsch was known as the 'Red Baron' – a name that was also applied to his VAH-4 Det Mike in *Enterprise* during the 1965-66 cruise. Wunsch returned as OinC of Det L in *Bon Homme Richard* in 1967, and during the cruise he showed an uncanny talent in the field of international relations.

When operating off the coast of Vietnam US naval vessels almost continuously had to deal with the presence of intelligence-gathering ships from the Soviet Union. Known by the naval term AGI, the vessels were usually based on seagoing fishing trawlers. They typically trailed the carriers while listening to communications and, it was assumed, passed intelligence to their North Vietnamese allies. The AGIs remained a pain in the rear throughout the war, but they had to be tolerated due to international law dealing with use of the sea. While some of the Soviet AGI captains stayed a respectful distance from US forces, others were much more aggressive and would steam their ship in a manner to harass the carrier and impede their attempts to conduct flight operations. These events would occasionally lead to hot flashes of the Cold War right there in the Gulf of Tonkin.

On one such day in July 1967 *Bon Homme Richard* was in the middle of recovering CVW-5 aircraft when the AGI cut across the ship's bow as Wunsch was turning final with his KA-3B. With collision at sea a distinct possibility, the carrier had no alternative but to make an immediate hard turn to pass behind the Soviet trawler. Wunsch, who was approaching the ramp, was given a wave-off by the LSOs (Landing Signal Officers) as his runway rapidly changed heading. He pushed the throttles as far forward as they would go, retracted the gear and speed brakes and stopped his rate of descent. Wunsch also saw the offending communist ship right off his nose, so he levelled off at about 100 ft and turned on the fuel dumps. Raw fuel poured from the wings and centreline as the 'Whale' overflew the trawler, covering it in JP-5.

The AGI reportedly went dead in the water as crews hurriedly broke out fire hoses to wash down their ship before a stray spark started a conflagration. They also decided to leave the carrier alone for the time being, and the 'Whale' subsequently recovered. Not surprisingly, the 'Red Baron' was an instant hero on the 'Bonnie Dick'.

By the start of 1968 the US Navy's Heavy Attack community was still centred at Whidbey Island, with VAH-2, -4, -8 and -10 pumping 'Whales' out to carriers on both coasts. There were still more than 160 A-3s of all varieties in the fleet, and VAH-123 continued as the RAG; filling ready rooms and maintenance shops for the Heavy Attack units, as well as VQ and VAP squadrons and the rapidly growing new EKA-3B community at Alameda. Significant changes, centered in Alameda, were coming though as the US Navy redefined what it needed from the Skywarrior.

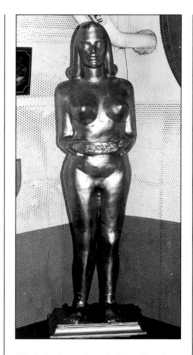

'Gigi', the legendary Golden Goddess, was photographed chained in the VAQ-131 ready room long after the unit's A-3 period, and probably not long prior to her mysterious final disappearance. Foul play was suspected (*US Navy*)

ALAMEDA AND JAMMERS

T he six-year period from 1968 to 1974 witnessed a dramatic change in the A-3B's primary role, with the end of Heavy Attack and the rise of an active EW community within Naval Aviation.

The US Navy had been ill prepared for the proliferation of SAMs in Vietnam, as its entire active EW (jamming) capability was centred in a small force of Douglas EA-1F Skyraiders (see *Osprey Combat Aircraft 77 – US Navy A-1 Skyraider Units of the Vietnam War*). As game as their crews were, the EA-1Fs did not possess either the aerodynamic or electronic capability to be truly effective against the rapidly expanding threat. Finding a replacement therefore became a critical priority.

The US Marine Corps had been the first service to deploy jet-powered jammers, as it had modified Korean War-era Douglas F3D Skyknight nightfighters into F3D-2Q (EF-10B) EW aircraft from 1955. Despite being fitted with a system little better than the one in the EA-1F, they performed inspired work deep into North Vietnam from the very start of the war. The EF-10B was in turn replaced by the very capable Grumman EA-6A Intruder from 1966. While the US Navy was intrigued by the 'Electric Intruder', it quickly looked beyond the two-seater to a proposed four-seat variant that would eventually become the EA-6B Prowler. While that was the obvious path to take, the service needed a more capable jamming platform sooner than the new Grumman programme would be available. Not surprisingly, the A-3 was more than ready and capable of taking on these duties.

In 1966 the 'Whale' depot at Alameda began conversion of the first A-3B into a combined jammer/tanker aircraft, designated the EKA-3B. The jet was initially described as a 'TACOS' ('Tanker-Countermeasures-Or-Strike') aircraft, although the ordnance capability was quickly deleted as the bomb-bay was now full of jammers and the bomb rake pinned shut. Within the fleet the 'TACOS' term did not last long either, the new type quickly being stuck with the predictable name 'Queer Whale'.

The heart of the EKA-3B was a battery of jammers and a dedicated operator who could modify jamming assignments as the tactical situation dictated. On top of this

The Douglas EA-1F was the US Navy's fleet jamming aircraft for the first three years of the Vietnam War, being replaced by the EKA-3B from mid-1967. This VAW-13 aircraft is being shot from *Coral Sea's* solitary waist catapult in 1966. The large wing pod is for the APS-31 radar, while the smaller pods contain ALT-2 jammers. A 300-gallon fuel tank is carried on the centreline. The aircraft also has a pair of 20 mm cannon installed in its wings, giving it a modicum of self-protection (*US Navy*)

VAW-13's second detachment to a modified-*Essex* class carrier was Det 19, which deployed in *Hancock* in July 1968. This photograph shows BuNo 142652/NP 843 at Alameda in June of that same year. Its Modex numbers would soon change to the 020 series, with this aircraft becoming NP 022. Once deployed, the det would add coloured rudders and lightning bolt tanker stripes. The jet exhibits the full EKA-3B configuration, with ALQ-92 side blisters and a single bomb-bay door that swung to starboard only with the ALT-27 canoe attached (*Bill Swisher via Tailhook Association*)

the aircraft also provided an excellent tanker capability for the air wing. The jet was normally crewed by three Naval Aviators, with the fourth 'jump seat' still available for an additional rider. Instead of an enlisted crewmember, the third position was usually occupied by an NFO who operated about two-thirds of the receiver and jamming systems. The aircraft weighed 44,000 lbs when empty – about 4000 lbs more than a 'straight' KA-3B. Fuel capacity was about four tons less due to the jamming gear in the bomb-bay area.

EW modifications included the addition of the ALT-27 jamming system, which consisted of a pair of steerable antennas in the E/F bands, as well as the Alpha-band (VHF) ALQ-92 system. While the ALT-27's antennas were covered by a new belly 'canoe' that faired into the refuelling store, the ALQ-92 had two distinct antenna arrays. One of the latter took the form of a single large vertically-polarised VHF blade antenna under the nose, its job being to jam North Vietnamese fighter control frequencies. The most obvious external additions to the EKA-3B were four large blisters on the sides of the fuselage that covered horizontally-polarised antennas for use against lower frequency early warning radars such as 'Knife Rest'.

In terms of frequency range and power output, the EKA-3Bs were considerably better than the EA-1Fs they replaced. Their much higher operational altitude also greatly increased the geographic area they could impact. While initially thinking that ten would be all that were required, the US Navy eventually converted 39 airframes.

When it came to deciding where to base the new 'Whales', the choice came down to either putting the modified aircraft into an established EW unit or assigning a new mission set to the Whidbey Heavy Attack community. In the end, the first path was taken, with Airborne Early Warning Squadron Thirteen (VAW-13) at NAS Alameda being given the job of introducing the EKA-3B to the fleet. The 'Zappers' had been established as VAW-13 at Agana, on Guam, in September 1959 as a sister unit to North Island-based VAW-11. Both squadrons provided AD-5W and AD-5Q aircraft for Airborne Early Warning (AEW) and EW dets, respectively, to Pacific Fleet carriers.

Two years later AirPac decided to split the EW and AEW roles, with VAW-13 moving to Alameda to become the Pacific Fleet's sole active ECM squadron by taking all of the force's AD-5Qs, while VAW-11's role became entirely carrier-based AEW with the 'Guppy Spads' and WF/E-1 Tracers. Between 1961 and 1968 VAW-13 kept a sizeable detachment of

'Fat Spads' at Cubi Point, from where they were supplied as dedicated jamming assets to carriers operating throughout Southeast Asia. The first EKA-3Bs joined the squadron in May 1967, and on 4 November Det 61 left California in *Ranger* for the war zone under the command of Lt Cdr Jim Ostergren, who had also been involved in most of the type's operational testing.

Getting its first detachments out of the door was not an easy task due to a lack of trained A-3 personnel and inadequate parts support. The initial plan was for aircrew and maintainers to come from the Whidbey RAG while the 'Zappers' conducted in-house EW training. Things started off slowly, however. There was also what has been described by one individual as 'passive resistance' within the ready room as the propeller crowd reluctantly gave way to jet-trained aviators – all this as they carried out a major change in aircraft types while supporting combat operations in-theatre.

Delays in getting the new EKA-3Bs and men ready led to a final EA-1F detachment leaving Alameda with *Kitty Hawk* in November 1967. Nonetheless, by April of the following year the squadron had successfully deployed four detachments with the new aircraft. By the start of 1968 VAW-13 had 15 EKA-3Bs and nine EA-1F assigned, as well as 130 officers and 625 enlisted men. The 'Fat Spads' were all gone by Thanksgiving, although the unit did retain a single A-1E for use as a squadron hack.

Among the men who made the transition from A-1 to A-3 was Carroll Beeler, a Naval Aviator and LSO. In January 2002 he compared waving both types, and while he considered the EA-1F to be very straightforward, he reported that 'the "Whale" was snotty on line up. You did not let the jet drift in close. A "right-for-lineup" call could result in a small pilot-induced oscillation, which would get the hook swinging and end up in a "Whale Dance" in the wires. In an extreme situation you could get an in-flight engagement, where both wingtips or nacelles could touch the deck as well. I remember one or two of these. Our pilots came from a lot of places – we had a former CH-46 driver and another who'd last flown C-54s. Their abilities were all over the scale.

A VAW-13 Det 31 'Killer Whale' EKA-3B spreads its wings and tail as it moves up to 'Bonnie Dick's' catapult two during the 1968 deployment. The tail, which could be isolated from the wing fold, was frequently left up. An A-4F from VA-212 and F-8s wait their turn for launch in the background. This was the first three-aircraft EKA-3B detachment to be embarked in a '27C' carrier (*US Navy*)

A VAW-13 Det 66 'Whale' launches from *America's* catapult three in 1968. The 'Zappers' provided three EKAs for this combat deployment and VAH-10 deployed a pair of KA-3Bs to form a joint five-'Whale' complement for CVW-6 (*US Navy*)

'On a "27C" [modified *Essex* class] the wingtip went right over the LSO's head. I had to jump into the net on an "OCLUIC" [LSO shorthand for "Over-Controlled Line-Up in Close"] where he came back at us. I pitched the pickle [waveoff] switch and the wingtip ripped it out of the console. I still have it as a keepsake.'

Beeler would later transition to F-8s and fly with VF-24 off *Hancock* until he was shot down by an SA-2 and captured on 24 May 1972 during Operation *Linebacker*. Released from a PoW camp in 1973, he would move to the Naval Reserves in 1978 and fly with McDonnell Douglas and General Electric as a test pilot, before joining Sino Swearingen Aircraft in 1997. On 26 April 2003 Beeler perished while conducting a test flight in an SJ30 business jet near San Antonio.

While AirPac had set the 'big deck' tanker requirement at five 'Whales', VAW-13 alone could not provide these numbers as EKA-3B transition and availability continued to be affected by the depot's completion rate of only three to four aircraft per month. Indeed, it would not be until late 1969 that the last of 39 jets was delivered for use. The solution was to fill in the first six deployments by teaming three VAW-13 EKA-3Bs with a pair of KA-3Bs from one of the Whidbey HATRONs. Lt Cdr Ostergren's Det 61 was joined by VAH-2, which established the practice where the two 'Whale' dets would be combined into a joint operation, with the senior OinC being the overall commander. Through to the end of 1968 six such blended dets would deploy to Southeast Asia.

The first 'small deck' detachment of three EKA-3Bs departed in January, with CVW-5 in *Bon Homme Richard*, as the self-styled 'Killer Whales'. Det 65, assigned to *Enterprise* with three jammers, had left Alameda earlier that same month, joining a pair of tankers from VAH-2. Det 66, with

VAH-10 as a teammate, was next, deploying in April with Norfolk-based *America* and CVW-6 for a war cruise. A month later 'Connie' headed back to the war with CVW-14 and a joint VAW-13/VAH-2 Det 64. VAW-13's last mixed detachment headed west in September 1968 in *Coral Sea* with two VAH-2 KA-3Bs. Only one more 'joint det' would be required, departing Alameda in October 1968 in *Ranger* while a major reorganisation was underway back at home that quickly made such an unwieldy arrangement unnecessary.

BIRTH OF THE VAQ COMMUNITY

By 1967 it had become obvious that the US Navy was going to end the A-3 Heavy Attack mission as it was known and instead emphasise the aircraft's tanking and jamming roles. The primary question became what form this change would take. In November 1967 the Chief of Naval Operations directed that three of the remaining Whidbey-based deploying Heavy Attack units (VAH-2, -4 and -10) be consolidated into one large squadron during the following summer, with VAH-2 being the surviving designation. COMFAIRWHIDBEY immediately went one step further and formally recommended that the unit be re-designated Aerial Refueling Squadron One (VK-1). Neither plan was carried out, however. Instead, the US Navy decided to form an entirely new community that would eventually be equipped with the new EA-6B, which was expected around 1971. In the meantime, the centre of the A-3's world would become Alameda.

Within the ranks of the US Navy's senior staff the need for a professional carrier-based EW force had finally been recognised. The rise in SAM systems and what would soon be described as an 'Integrated Air Defense System' (IADS) drove the decision to separate the jamming mission from its long association with the VAW community and establish Tactical Electronic Warfare Squadrons (VAQ) as distinct entities. To do this the service followed the path it had only recently taken with the VAW community, where the single E-1/E-2 squadrons on each coast (VAW-11 and -12) became the basis for individual units, and new wings to control them.

One of the first moves was to disestablish VAH-8, which 'folded its tent' at Whidbey on 17 January 1968. During its tenure the 'Fireballers' had made eight major WestPacs in *Midway* and *Constellation*, always as a full squadron. The next move involved VAW-33, the AirLant EA-1F unit base at NAS Quonset Point, Rhode Island. The 'Knight Hawks' were re-designated as VAQ-33 on 1 February 1968 and remained a 'Spad' squadron until 1970, when it became the first 'electronic adversary' unit within the new Fleet Electronic Warfare Support Group (FEWSG).

Out on the west coast VAW-13 was re-designated VAQ-130 on 1 October 1968, while keeping the 'Zapper' title, 23 EKA-3Bs, six

VAW-13 was assigned the VR tailcode when established in 1959, and it retained the marking through re-designation as VAQ-130 in 1968. Several of the early EKA-3B detachments carried it on cruise too, including Det 34 in *Oriskany*. However, after starting the 1969 deployment with VR on its jets, the det soon switched to CVW-19's NM tailcode. All three of Det 34's aircraft are shown here prior to the cruise with tanker stripes applied – something the 'Zappers' were not well known for. The fourth aircraft in line, KA-3B BuNo 138929, was not part of the det. It would subsequently crash at NAS Patuxent River, Maryland, on 26 January 1979 while flying at the Naval Air Test Center (*US Navy via Tailhook Association*)

VAH-4 was re-designated VAQ-131 in November 1968 and duly moved to Alameda, where it gained EKA-3Bs. Seven weeks later the unit deployed with CVW-11 in *Kitty Hawk*. Initially using single-digit Modex numbers, it soon moved to the new AirPac standard 610 series for VAQ units. BuNo 142403 shows the unit's modified Heavy Four insignia and tail trim, as well as the ultimate expression of tanker stripes (*Bill Swisher via Tailhook Association*)

Bon Homme Richard is seen underway in the Gulf of Tonkin in 1969, having CVW-5 embarked for the veteran carrier's next-to-last deployment. A pair of VAQ-130 Det 31 EKA-3Bs are present on the flightdeck, along with Skyhawks from VA-22, VA-94 and VA-144 and Crusaders from VF-51, VF-53 and VFP-63. The carrier's C-1 COD has been chained down alongside the island (*US Navy via Tailhook Association*)

detachments and six remaining A-1s. The new 130 series established the sequence for all following fleet EW squadrons and, eventually, the EA-6B community.

A new Type Commander, Tactical Electronic Warfare Wing Thirteen (VAQWING-13), was established under COMFAIRALAMEDA in September 1968 to administratively control what would quickly become a busy community. Capt Don Monday, a highly experienced A-3 pilot, was named its first Commodore, with a staff of six officers and two enlisted sailors.

The 'Zappers' would not be alone on the Alameda ramp for long, as the US Navy planned for six additional five-aircraft VAQ squadrons for larger ships, while keeping VAQ-130 as a detachment provider for smaller decks. This growth also greatly increased the career potential for Naval Aviators assigned to a field that had, up to now, been largely considered a 'dead end' assignment.

First impacted were VAH-4 and -2, which were re-designated VAQ-131 and -132 on 1 November 1968 and moved to California to join VAQ-130. There was no rest as the operational tempo demanded that both units get up to speed immediately. Indeed, VAQ-131 joined CVW-11 in *Kitty Hawk* for a nine-month deployment only seven weeks after moving to Alameda. According to one former squadron member, the unit did not have time to deal with things like a new title or insignia, so they modified

VAH-4's logo and used their radio call-sign, 'Holly Green', as their nickname. It was assigned three EKA-3Bs and a pair of KA-3Bs, as were the units that followed.

With more time available to make the transition, VAQ-132 adopted a new moniker, 'Scorpions', as well as appropriate insignia. It left California for Vietnam in *Enterprise* with CVW-9 in January 1969. Three more squadrons followed during the course of the year, with VAQ-130 detachments as their core. On 4 March VAQ-133 was

VAH-123. The 'Vikings' of Heavy 10 had become the preferred provider of KA-3 detachments to Atlantic Fleet carriers from 1965, with three dets (in *Franklin D Roosevelt*, *Forrestal* and *America*) also seeing combat in Southeast Asia. In September 1968 the squadron absorbed three VAH-2 detachments whilst they were underway in-theatre, doubling the size of the squadron. By 1 January 1969 the unit's authorised strength was 18 KA-3Bs, 65 officers and 695 troops. A small number of EKA-3Bs arrived the following month, making the 'Vikings' the only VAH unit to fly the type. The EKAs would deploy with Det 60 to the Med with CVW-3 in *Saratoga* the following July, thus giving the 'Queer Whale' its operational debut with Sixth Fleet.

Finally, on 1 September 1970, VAH-10 were re-designated VAQ-129 – one digit under 130, but a re-numbering rich in significance as it joined the 120-series occupied by AirPac training squadrons. The ultimate plan was that the unit would become the RAG for the new EA-6B 'Super Intruder' due to reach the fleet in 1971.

VAH-10's KA-3B detachments that were underway in USS *Shangri-La* (CVS-38) and *Independence* made the change at sea and returned home with the new designation. Det 38 involved three KA-3Bs with CVW-8 off Vietnam, CVS-38 operating as an attack carrier during its final deployment. This was the only time an Atlantic Fleet '27C' deployed with 'Whales'.

Only one more 'Whale' detachment would leave Whidbey, Det 19 departing Oak Harbor with three EKA-3Bs in October 1970. It duly became the only full deployment ever sent out under the VAQ-129 title.

On 1 February 1971 the last Heavy Attack unit in the US Navy, VAH-123, was disestablished, as the replacement training duties for all A-3s were moved to VAQ-130, which added TA-3Bs to its stable for the

'Whale' recovery. VAQ-132's KA-3B NG 611 approaches the ramp on *America* during the ship's 1970 cruise, its progress being watched by a yellow shirt who is apparently standing *inside* the foul deck line! The amount of smoke being produced by the J57s gave the LSOs a good clue as to the aircraft's power setting (*US Navy*)

VAQ-133 was established in March 1969 using VAQ-130 Det 64 as a core. The unit's first deployment, with three EKA-3Bs (including this aircraft) and a pair of KA-3Bs, commenced in August 1969 in *Constellation* with CVW-14. After a second trip to Vietnam (with CVW-11 aboard *Kitty Hawk*) in 1970-71, the unit moved to Whidbey for EA-6B transition, where it became known as the 'Wizards' (*Bill Swisher via Rich Dann*)

job. The ceremony at Whidbey's hangar five featured TA-3B NJ 327 being towed out one end as the unit's final orders were read. Moments later the base's first EA-6B (BuNo 158029/TR 01) taxied into the hangar from the other side, representing its arrival at VAQ-129. An era had truly passed in the US Navy, ending roughly 12 years of A-3 training at Whidbey. During this time the squadron had produced 555 pilots, 625 B/Ns and 464 enlisted aircrew, as well as having functioned as the AirPac A-6 RAG in 1966-67.

Although VAQWING-13 transferred north on 1 October 1970 in anticipation of the new aircraft arriving, it still retained administrative control of the Alameda VAQ units. The move placed it under the control of COMFAIRWHIDBEY, which also covered AirPac's six A-6 units. The plan was now to start moving squadrons up to Washington State for conversion as quickly as practical. The real exodus from Alameda began when VAQ-132, which had returned home from Southeast Asia just in time for Christmas 1970, was moved without equipment to Whidbey to become the first fleet EA-6B outfit. The 'Holly Green' of VAQ-131 was next, in May 1971. VAQ-133 and -134 followed during the summer of that same year, both units having completed two 'Whale' cruises each.

This left just the 'Zappers' and 'Homebrew' at Alameda to finish out the EKA-3B's service. VAQ-130 continuing as the RAG while working four sea-going detachments. VAQ-135 had made only one cruise, in *Coral Sea*, as a complete five-aircraft squadron before becoming a detachment provider. By the end of 1971 it had five teams, two of which deployed to the Mediterranean with *Franklin D Roosevelt* and USS *John F Kennedy* (CVA-67). Squadron lore relates that it would be Det 2 in *Forrestal* that in 1972 coined the term 'Black Raven' as an identity, which quickly became VAQ-135's nickname – it has since lasted for more than 40 years.

Unit movement led to significant personnel changes as well. While some men jumped at the chance to fly the new aircraft, which would soon be christened Prowler, many remained at Alameda and continued flying 'Whales'. Among the latter was Dick Damron. He returned from his 1971 deployment with VAQ-134 as the squadron moved its flag to Whidbey Island for EA-6B transition, while the majority of its personnel were redistributed to other units at Alameda. Damron transferred to VAQ-135 and was assigned to Det 5, which deployed in February 1972 with CVW-21 in *Hancock*. With only three EKA-3Bs assigned, the det operated in a significantly altered fashion from Damron's first deployment. With a smaller deck and a considerably different attitude about EW in the air wing, the det started working out of Cubi Point and then Da Nang, which is where it spent most of its war. Over the next seven months, most of Damron's flights would start and finish on the beach. He would end up flying 250 combat hours, yet trap on the boat only 34 times.

The new squadrons lost five aircraft between 1968 and 1971. On 2 December 1968 the 'Scorpions'' KA-3B BuNo 138909 suffered a bizarre failure while taking a shot off *Enterprise's* catapult 1 during workups. About one-third of the way down the cat stroke the nose gear rose off the flightdeck and the tyre exploded. The gear collapsed, pieces came off the nose and the bridle disengaged, with the 'Whale' leaving the bow nose down, impacting the water. ADJ2 Walt Kaess managed to escape and was recovered, but Lt(jg) Tom Masten and ATC Richard Edwards were killed.

The 'Homebrew' lost their first 'Whale' on 16 May 1970 when BuNo 142657/NL 613 crashed off the coast of South Vietnam. The aircraft had been on a ferry flight from Cubi Point to *Coral Sea* in the Gulf when it was forced to divert to Da Nang. No sign of Cdr Richard Skeen, Lt Cdr Gene McNally or ADCS Ed Conner was ever found. Less than two months later, on 4 July, the 'Scorpions' lost a second EKA-3B in yet another unusual mishap when BuNo 142400/NG 614 had its drag chute deploy during a bolter off *America*. Unable to maintain flying speed, the aircraft settled into the water, with all three crew being successfully recovered.

VAQ-131 wrote off EKA-3B BuNo 142252/AB 615 on 7 August 1970 while returning from a work-up period on the east coast. The aircraft had been leading two squadronmates climbing through heavy weather from Buckley ANGB, in Denver, Colorado, when it pitched up, stalled and lost control. All four men onboard bailed out, two suffering frostbite from long parachute rides through freezing rain. Indeed, the pilot and B/N barely made it, coming down about 50 ft from the aircraft wreckage. Although injured, both would later command EA-6B squadrons.

Sometimes aircraft losses were hard to explain. VAQ-130 Det 3, off *Oriskany*, had BuNo 147649/NM 619 crash into the Gulf of Tonkin on 18 June 1971 after tanking F-8Js. One of the fighter pilots reported the 'Whale' had completed the event and detached from the Crusaders by starting what was described as a barrel-roll manoeuvre. When the aircraft was inverted at the top of its roll the nose suddenly dropped into the near vertical. It held that position until impact with the water, killing pilot Lt John Painter, B/N Lt(jg) Ray DeBlasio and ADJ2 Barry Bidwell. The mishap was remarkable enough to draw the ire of the US Navy's irascible 'Grampaw Pettibone' in his April 1972 column printed in *Naval Aviation News*. 'Pettibone', which was actually written by a Naval Aviator on the staff of the Navy Safety Center, cited the 'Whale' pilot for the loss, specifically by violating NATOPS and putting his aircraft in a dangerous and unrecoverable situation.

ENDGAME

The invasion of South Vietnam on 29 March 1972 changed the entire complexion of the war, with US Navy aircraft quickly mounting strikes deep into the North that saw them having to run the gauntlet of a defensive network that had been given three years to improve. Four

VAQ-130 Det 1 thought it was heading home in March 1972 after six months in the war zone when the invasion of South Vietnam changed CVA-64's cruise schedule. What followed was a further three months in-theatre, performing what CVW-9 called 'Cruise Bravo'. EKA-3B BuNo 147658/NG 616 is shown about to trap on *Constellation* during that deployment (*US Navy via Rich Dann*)

carriers were in-theatre, all of which carried EKA-3Bs. The 'Homebrew' covered three of the decks, with Dets 1, 3 and 5 on *Kitty Hawk, Coral Sea and Hancock*. Up in Japan, *Constellation* was preparing to head home with VAQ-130 Det 1, but it was hurriedly ordered to return to *Yankee Station* to join the effort.

With strikes now going back inland, 'Whales' continued to work off the beach, normally staying about 20 miles from North Vietnam so as to be out of the maximum range of coastal SA-2 sites. It could be quite a show on some nights, with one VAQ-130 EWO later recalling that they would know where the strike group was by watching the AAA and SAM trails through the air.

Dick Damron was in-theatre at this time. 'The spring invasion led to a greatly increased ops tempo, with most flights lasting two to three hours, typically starting and ending at Da Nang. We ended up supporting every carrier over there, although it was almost all from the beach.

'Aircraft were stressed and we had lots of parts issues as little quirks of the "Whale" manifested themselves. For example, the engine fire warning lights had a disconcerting habit of illuminating right after takeoff if it had recently rained. This became such a common occurrence that it got to the point where you simply ignored the fire light when it did indeed come on right after takeoff following a rain storm. You just confirmed visually you weren't on fire and continued on your mission, figuring the light would go out eventually.'

Damron later moved on to EA-6Bs and deployed with VAQ-133, being one of the few Naval Aviators who flew all three of the US Navy's EW platforms of the period. He retired from the service in 1983 and went on to enjoy a highly successful career in business, working at one time or another with Lockheed, Northrop and Boeing, as well as serving as a vice president at Litton.

The initial offensive against North Vietnamese targets, designated Operation *Freedom Train*, gave way to full-out strikes from 10 May in what was now called Operation *Linebacker*. *Midway*, with CVW-5 and VAQ-130 Det 2 onboard, joined the effort, placing five flightdecks in-theatre. Once again, jamming aircraft proved vital for support. The criticality of properly executed electronic warfare, and the skill of the EKA-3B NFOs, was not always obvious to the rest of the air wing. Sometimes, however, their work saved lives in dramatic fashion, as exhibited by a story from *Constellation*.

The day of 10 May 1972 would go down as the most memorable of the Vietnam air war, at least in terms of MiG kills. Phantom IIs ranging from Seventh Fleet carriers were credited with eight MiGs during the course of the day.

Lt Curt Dosé was an F-4J pilot with VF-92 onboard *Constellation* during *Linebacker*. On the morning of the epic 10 May air battles he and his back-seater, Lt Jim McDevitt (a former A-3 B/N) started things off by shooting down a MiG-21 over Kep airfield. For their second flight of the day they drew an *Iron Hand* escort mission for a VA-146 A-7E near Haiphong in support of a CVW-9 strike that would lead to several more MiGs being destroyed. The story is best told by 'Dozo' Dosé;

'About 20 nautical miles out we accelerated ahead of the Alpha Strike to a covering position over Haiphong Harbour. The sun was low and there was a hazy 5000 ft undercast obscuring most of the ground. We were orbiting at about 11,000 ft when I started getting SAM search signals. I called "Busy Bee" [the A-7] and he had nothing. I then got SAM acquisition signals and notified "Busy Bee". He still had nothing. When I got SAM launch indications I took the lead and called for a break left into the missile. Two SA-2s in echelon burst out of the undercast, having already dropped their boosters. I pushed my nose over with negative-G to check their targeting, and both SAMs nodded down – they were both on me. I pulled 7Gs up and into them, but it was too late. They were tracking straight for us at Mach 2. Not only would they shoot us down, but their ball bearing warheads would explode directly into our cockpit.

'I watched the missile's small canards making final corrections and prepared to die, but they did not detonate. The lead SA-2 flew five feet over our canopy and the second flew 20 ft in front of our nose. I had an 8 mm

EKA-3Bs had their ALQ-92 gear removed from late 1972, with the most obvious result being the loss of the four large fuselage blisters. The type retained the ALT-27 package installed in the bomb-bay, however, as BuNo 142659 shows at Alameda on 11 May 1973. It also wears the 'Black Raven's' attractive markings, as well as the TR tailcode that had been assigned to VAQW-13 and was carried by many VAQ-130/135 'Whales' and VAQ-129 EA-6Bs during this period. BuNo 142659 would be converted into a KA-3B and eventually destroyed on 10 July 1977 whilst serving with VAQ-308 (*Clay Janssen via Angelo Romano*)

movie camera strapped below the APR-25, shooting forward, and the second SAM can be clearly seen on the film flying full frame from left to right. I rolled right and watched the two SAMs continue straight past us, upward above the setting sun. They never did go off. I told "Busy Bee" that I had the lead and we were exiting the area. I had had 15-20 SAMs shot at my aeroplane in Vietnam, but these were the closest I had ever seen.

'We returned to the ship and landed. We walked down to IOIC [Integrated Operational Intelligence Center] to debrief and waited for a debriefer. The "Queer" A-3 crew [an EKA-3B from VAQ-130 Det 1] was already debriefing, and I heard them say that there were so many SAMs in the air that they couldn't jam the guidance, so they switched to jamming the fusing. The time matched up with our save, and it was clear that these guys were why my SAMs had not fused and detonated – and killed Jim and me. I took that EKA-3 crew half a case of Vodka that night – all I had left for the line period. I then rejoined our VF-92 party celebrating our MiG kill and mourning our losses [VF-92 had lost its XO, Cdr Henry Blackburn, and his RIO, Lt Stephen Rudloff, to AAA – both men safely ejected and Rudloff became a PoW, but Blackburn is presumed to have been killed either during or soon after capture]. That's the way it was.'

Linebacker I continued, with EKA-3Bs providing 100 per cent of the carrier-based jamming capability until mid-June, when *America*/CVW-8 arrived with the first EA-6B Prowlers to deploy. These jets belonged to VAQ-132, which had gone through transition at Whidbey in 1971. The new 'station wagon' version of the A-6 Intruder (with room for 'Mom, Dad and the kids') featured four seats and the new ALQ-99 tactical jamming system, and it marked the beginning of the end for the EKA-3B, as transition to the new type would take only three years to complete. While actually a tad slower than the 'Whale', and shorter ranged, the EA-6B had a better jamming and receiver system than the EKA-3B, as well as being considered much more survivable. It also had the obvious benefit of being in production, which would last for almost 20 years as 170 Prowlers eventually rolled off the Grumman line.

The renewed offensive in December, now called *Linebacker II*, featured five US Navy jamming squadrons – two with Prowlers (*America*'s VAQ-132

The view from the receiver. A VF-21 F-4J has its probe extended prior to plugging into the basket trailed by a VAQ-130 Det 4 EKA-3B off California in April 1974. A few weeks later the det would be pulled from CVW-2 prior to *Ranger*'s deployment and the 'Zappers' would head north for EA-6B transition (*Lt(jg) Jan Jacobs*)

and *Enterprise*-based VAQ-131, which now called itself the 'Lancers'). Three 'Zapper' dets were on the line as well, with Det 3 in *Oriskany*, Det 4 in *Ranger* and *Midway's* Det 2 still on what would be an interminable 327-day deployment. These are the units that finished the last part of the war, all being present when the cease-fire took effect on 23 January 1973.

The final major mishap involving an EKA-3B had occurred just 48 hours earlier when 'Zapper' Det 4's BuNo 142634/NE 611 lost its starboard engine during a cat shot from *Ranger* shortly before midnight. The aircraft went into the water, and Lt Cdr Charlie Parker, Lt(jg) Keith Christophersen and PO Richard Wiehr were all killed.

One more 'Homebrew' detachment, Det 2, arrived in *Coral Sea* in March and took part in Operation *End Sweep* and other 'clean-up' missions. By this time the aircraft were losing their distinctive side blisters as their ALQ-92 gear was removed. VAQ-135 Det 5, calling themselves the 'Hamburgers of WestPac', arrived with *Hancock*/CVW-21 in May 1973. They would be the squadron's final team to head west in 'Whales', as the unit's CO, now Cdr Tom Maxwell, was ordered to expedite movement of VAQ-135 to Whidbey for EA-6B transition. Its two deployed detachments (3 and 5) were both transferred to VAQ-130 (as Dets 2 and 5), which remained at Alameda as the last EKA-3B operator.

The final Mediterranean cruise for a bomber 'Whale' ended in January 1974 with the return of VAQ-130 Det 1 from a nine-month journey that had seen it cross-deck from *John F Kennedy* to *Independence* in order to keep an EW platform deployed in-theatre. On the west coast, 'Zapper' Det 3, in *Oriskany* with CVW-19, chopped to the Seventh Fleet in October 1973 and returned home in June 1974. It proved to be the last EKA-3B detachment to cruise, Det 3 flying the last bomb-bay equipped A-3s to make a major deployment.

The end of the road came for the EKA-3B in May 1974 when VAQ-130 was alerted that it would move immediately to Whidbey Island for transition to the Prowler. Most affected was Lt Cdr Bob Weber's Det 4, which was working up for a deployment with CVW-2 in *Ranger*. It was pulled from the wing a few days prior to its departure from San Diego and the ship/wing team made its subsequent WestPac sans EW support as the 'Zappers' headed north.

The reserves at Alameda flew 'Whales' from 1970 through to 1989, with two squadrons providing tanking support for their CVWRs and regular US Navy units. Here, a KA-3B from VAQ-308 works with a section of VF-301 F-4Ns off San Diego in May 1978. BuNo 142664/ND 632 was one of the former EKA-3Bs converted back to KA-3B configuration for Reserve use. A year later the unit would be re-designated as a tanker (VAK) squadron (*Lt Cdr Jan Jacobs*)

The EKA-3B had proven to be an interim aircraft that provided roughly seven years of service between the EA-1F and EA-6B, doing everything the US Navy had asked of it. The remaining airframes were either stripped of all EW gear and re-designated as KA-3Bs for service with the reserves or sent into well-earned retirement within the Military Aircraft Storage and Disposal Center (MASDC) at Davis-Monthan AFB in Arizona. The aircraft's impact and influence would be felt in the EA-6B community in the form of the men who had flown the 'Whale' in combat, and who would lead the US Navy's VAQ squadrons for several years to come.

'WHALES' FOR THE RESERVES

In 1970 the US Navy Reserve completely re-organised its aviation units after what could only be described as a year-long fiasco. In 1968 President Lyndon B Johnson had ordered a major re-call of USAF and US Navy reserve units in response to the seizure of USS *Pueblo* (AGER-2) by the North Koreans. While the USAF was able to quickly mobilise and send several Air National Guard units to Vietnam, the US Navy's reserve component was unable to deploy any of its tactical units, flying F-8s and A-4s, to active carriers in 1969.

While the full story remains contentious for a variety of reasons (and certainly not because of issues with the Reservists themselves), the fact was the US Navy was embarrassed by its inability to use the force. It duly came to the conclusion that the numerous reserve units scattered across the country had to be reorganised into a more responsive organisation that was much closer in capability to the frontline force. The answer was to form two new Reserve Carrier Air Wings (CVWR), with squadrons aligned more closely with regular US Navy units. This meant supplying reserve squadrons units with more modern aircraft, and then giving them realistic training. The result was CVWR-20 and -30, and among the F-8s, A-4s and E-1s in the air wings were two new A-3 units based in Alameda.

In spite of their designations, the 'Jockeys' of VAQ-208 (established on 31 July 1970) and 'Griffons' of VAQ-308 (established on 2 May 1970) never received EKA-3Bs and were typically assigned four or five KA-3Bs. Both units would be heavily involved with both air wings in the tanker and high-speed transport roles for the next 19 years. Between 1970 and 1973 they supported combat operations in Southeast Asia from Cubi Point and Atsugi as tankers and 'fast-CODs', delivering supplies, mail and personnel to ships on *Yankee Station* whilst carrying out the latter role. In December 1971 VAQ-308 would also support the short visit by *Enterprise* into the Indian Ocean as part of the US response to the Indo-Pakistan War.

In October 1973, during Operation *Nickel Grass*, the Reserve's 'Whales' were critical in providing fuel for a wave of A-4 Skyhawks flown to Israel during the Yom Kippur War. In this case their KA-3Bs, flying from *John F Kennedy* and *Franklin D Roosevelt*, enabled the A-4s to bypass countries that were not allowing support for the embattled Jewish state.

By the late 1970s it had become obvious that both units were never going to be true electronic warfare squadrons, so they were re-designated as TANKRONS VAK-208 and -308 on 1 October 1979. They would continue to provide exemplary service through to their disestablishment on 20 September 1989.

VAP AND VQ

While the A3D quickly took on the Heavy Attack role, the airframe's inherent versatility soon led to the US Navy developing the aircraft into three special-mission configurations for other purposes. These designs were collectively known within the Skywarrior community as 'versions', with the bomb-bay area being used for crew or equipment. Not simply modified bombers, they were delivered from the factory as significantly different airframes that required separate NATOPS manuals and qualifications for operation.

The 'versions' were flown in the fleet by two less-noted sub-communities, Fleet Air Reconnaissance (VQ) and Heavy Photo (VAP), who flew some of the more important, dangerous and little documented Skywarrior missions of the Vietnam War.

The 'versions' had significantly different fuselage sections than the bombers, with their bodies modified to carry additional aircrew or equipment. They also featured modified bleed-air systems that resulted in their ATMs being located side-by-side under the cockpit, with an exhaust on either side of the nose. Their emergency electrical system used a deployable Ram Air Turbine (replacing batteries in the bomber variant) that could be popped out the starboard side of the nose.

A more complex pressurisation system, required for the larger cabin, led to beefed-up canopy framing as well as replacement of the large, sliding upper escape hatch by a much smaller, inward-opening square door on top of the canopy. The addition of a pressurised crew compartment in the fuselage also required the use of only a single entry hatch, which was much more robust than that on the bombers because it was now the pressure seal.

A 'version' in flight. An RA-3B soars through a cirrus backdrop as streamers come off its wingtips in this beautiful photograph (*US Navy via Rich Dann*)

The A3D-2Q first flew in October 1958 and deployed in early 1960 to the US Navy's two Fleet Air Reconnaissance (VQ) squadrons, VQ-1 with the Pacific Fleet and VQ-2 operating with the Atlantic Fleet. They replaced interim A3D-1Q airframes modified from bombers, where the cockpits were altered to hold a fourth crewman and electronic support measures (ESM) systems were carried in the bomb-bay. Both units flew strategic reconnaissance missions along the periphery of the Soviet Union, China and Cuba. Many of these events were carried out as part of the Peacetime Aerial Reconnaissance Program (PARPRO), which directly supported activities of various national agencies.

While many references state that the EA-3B (as the A3D-2Q was re-designated in September 1962) was used for radar and communications jamming off Vietnam, that was actually not the case as the type carried no active jamming gear during the conflict. The error undoubtedly came from people confusing it with the EKA-3B. However, in the Mediterranean, VQ-2 was known to carry ALQ-31 jammers and chaff pods on wing stations to provide training for air wing fighters, particularly when other EW aircraft were not available in-theatre due to the Vietnam War.

The role of the EA-3B in Vietnam was strictly electronic reconnaissance against both radar and communications systems used by the enemy. As stated in the unit's official history, 'Specific types of support provided by the VQ-1 aircrews were MiG and SAM warning services, electronic order of battle updating and electronic intelligence collection in support of combat contingency planning'.

Along with the three seats in front were four men in the fuselage – usually one NFO and three enlisted – who performed the specialised ESM mission while seated lineally down the fuselage facing equipment panels on the port side of the aircraft. In order to facilitate rapid egress by the back-end crew the EA-3B had an additional upper escape hatch as well as a bail-out door in the starboard side of the fuselage that could be blown open if the need arose. The side door was not used for entry (as noted by some authors), but intended for emergency egress only.

VQ-1

The 'World Watchers' of VQ-1 were initially based at Yokota, in Japan, and moved to Guam in 1971. The unit's Atlantic fleet counterpart, VQ-2

'Launch "Whales!"' The catapult officer touches the deck as VQ-1 EA-3B 'Deep Sea 14' prepares to be shot from *Franklin D Roosevelt* during CVA-42's solitary combat cruise to Vietnam in 1966, while two VAH-10 Det 42 A-3Bs wait their turn. Note that only two of the three JBD panels are up due to the aircraft's length (*US Navy*)

'Bats', was found at Rota, in Spain. Both units were necessarily large squadrons, VQ-1 having 75 officers and 440 men assigned to maintain and fly both land-based Lockheed EC-121K 'Warning Stars' (and, eventually, EP-3B Orions) and carrier-based EA-3Bs. While the squadron worked closely with Seventh Fleet in a tactical strike-support role, it also conducted work similar to the USAF's 55th Strategic Reconnaissance Wing with its RB-47Hs and RC-135s.

While it had been monitoring North Vietnam intermittently since 1962, VQ-1 established a semi-permanent detachment at Da Nang early in the war. The unit operated both EC-121s and EA-3Bs from this location, typically flying off the coast of North Vietnam and over Laos to observe and record the electronic environment, while also providing threat warnings to strike aircraft going 'over the beach'.

A VQ-1 EA-3B, launched off *Ticonderoga*, was overhead for the initial Gulf of Tonkin incident on 2 August 1964. Carrier operations were almost continuous for the duration of the war, with the squadron probably operating off of every flightdeck that launched combat missions with Seventh Fleet.

While enlisted crewmen for the EA-3Bs were normally rated as Cryptological Technicians (CTs, or 'Crippies'), the seats could also be occupied by non-US Navy personnel – typically from the US Army, or other agencies, who were usually picked for their unique linguistic or technical abilities. The use of men unfamiliar with tactical flying occasionally led to a predictable amount of good-natured 'hazing'. One of the more popular routines was to brief that if the crew was required to bail out, the 'guest' operator would be the first to go down the chute 'in order to clear out all of the antennas on the belly so that the rest of us would survive'. It is reported that some visitors took the brief at face value and were not terribly amused.

Among the men who flew the EA-3B in Vietnam was Dave Ouellette, a 1965 graduate of the University of South Florida who earned his NFO wings in July 1966. Ouellette was ordered to VQ-2 at Rota and became qualified as an Evaluator (Eval) in both the Skywarrior and Warning Star. In late October 1968 he was sent to the Pacific on temporary duty as a member of VQ-2 Det B, which supplied two aircraft and crews to the war effort from 1965 through to 1969;

Lt(jg) Dave Ouellette, VQ-1 Eval, at Da Nang in 1968 (*Dave Ouellette*)

VQ-1 EA-3B BuNo 146457/PR 5 was photographed by Lt(jg) Dave Ouellette during his 1968 trip to the war zone. It displays the low-key squadron markings of the period. Although assigned the radio call-sign 'Deep Sea', VQ-1 was also widely known as 'Peter Rabbit' from its tailcode. Initially put on display in front of the Bachelor Officers' Quarters at Rota following its retirement from VQ-2 in 1991, BuNo 146457 was subsequently transferred to the Patriots Point Museum in Mount Pleasant, South Carolina, and craned onboard USS *Yorktown* (CVS-10) as an exhibit in April 2011 (*Dave Ouellette*)

'Peter Rabbit 6' again, this time waving off on *Coral Sea* in December 1966. Although the tailhook is still extended, the speed brakes are retracted and the pilot is holding his altitude, before making a turn downwind for another pass (*US Navy via Tailhook Association*)

'We normally flew with a full crew of seven in the "Whale" – three officers [a pilot, navigator and the Eval] and four enlisted. Position No 3, behind the pilot, was purely a plane captain seat. Later, when we went to the "Seawing" configuration, it became the communications spot. The positions in the fuselage were, from front to rear, numbered four through seven. No 4 was comms, No 5 had high bands, No 6 middle bands and No 7 was the Evaluator, who monitored the entire frequency range. These guys were amazing – at the top of their games, and enormously proficient.'

'Eggs' Ouellette remarked that during his first tour of Vietnam, when the bombing halt was in place, things were actually rather quiet. He would return to VQ-1 in October 1972, just in time for *Linebacker II*. During this tour he flew in all three squadron aircraft, the EP-3B having joined VQ-1 in the interim. While they did operate out of Da Nang, a lot of the det's work was from Cubi Point, which, in a 'Whale', frequently involved trapping on a carrier for fuel prior to flying a second mission, which ended back in the Philippines.

Lt(jg) T J Williams was a 1966 graduate of the Naval Academy who began his naval career as a 'black shoe' assigned to the destroyer USS *Collett* (DD-730) on a tour that included five-inch 'gun-fights' off the North Vietnamese coast with shore batteries. His transit to a physical examination for flight duty involved a January 1967 helicopter ride from his 'tin can' to a CVS. After being picked up by a helicopter, they were diverted to retrieve an A-4 pilot who had ejected off the beach. The pilot was dead in the water when they arrived, and Williams remembers watching over the body of the Naval Aviator in the cabin as they headed for the carrier. He passed the physical and was assigned to NFO training, subsequently graduating at the top of his class.

During Williams' time on a destroyer he had become fascinated with electronic warfare, and so he asked for orders to the VQ community. After a short stint at A-3 RAG VAH-123 as a navigator trainee, he was moved to Atsugi, where he joined VQ-1 and was quickly sent to Vietnam as part of an EA-3B crew;

'We were typically in-theatre for six weeks and then rotated back home to fly ParPro [Peacetime Airborne Reconnaissance Program] missions out of Japan. What a welcome to Southeast Asia though! Our first night in Da Nang [29 September 1968] we were rocketed and a VQ-2 bird "loaned" to VQ-1 (BuNo 144848) was heavily damaged. The unit tried to send her back to Japan on a ship for repair but the aircraft went overboard in heavy seas and was lost.

'At that time we normally flew the EA-3Bs at night while our "Willie Victors" [EC-121Ks] took the day shift. We'd typically brief at about 2200 hrs, launch around midnight and recover at Da Nang by 0500 hrs, so tanking was not normally required. We were doing a lot of support for A-6 strikes as well as for Special Operations teams. We also flew off carriers as needed, usually to work with the strikers.

'Things could be tedious as well, particularly after the bombing halt. The threat order of battle didn't really change much so things quickly became routine to the point that my pilot would let me fly the aircraft while on track. In doing so I eventually became proficient in all aspects of flying the "Whale", which proved providential on a mission when the pilot became incapacitated shortly after takeoff and I flew the rest of the mission as both pilot and navigator. Regardless of who was flying, precise navigation was required to enable a meaningful post-flight analysis of intelligence by the EW crew.'

By January 1969 VQ-1 had 12 EA-3Bs and six EC-121Ks assigned. Many of the NFOs and enlisted aircrewmen flew both types of aircraft. Williams states that one week he could be in Da Nang and the next flying Soviet ICBM monitoring missions out of Shemya, Alaska, with US Army specialists onboard.

When the North Koreans shot down a squadron EC-121K (BuNo 135749/PR 21) on 15 April 1969 Williams was assigned to a det onboard *Enterprise*, which moved up off Korea for any potential reprisal. 'We lost 31 men in that aircraft. About 11 months later another squadron "Willie Victor" (BuNo 145927/PR 26) crashed at Da Nang, with 23 of the 31 onboard being killed. The loss of 54 men in less than a year must be a

VQ-1 EA-3B BuNo 146451/PR 2 sits at Da Nang in 1968. Nose details include the square ATM exhaust featured on all of the Skywarrior versions and the starboard escape hatch unique to the EA and TA types. The belly entry hatch was also substantially bigger on the tankers than on the bombers since it acted as a pressure seal for the entire aircraft (*Dave Ouellette*)

VQ-1 EA-3B BuNo 142671/PR 6 flies with an F-4B from VF-114 off *Kitty Hawk* during the carrier's 1965-66 combat cruise (*US Navy*)

record among US squadrons since World War 2'.

During the war VQ-1 quietly pioneered new tactics to deal with the rapidly evolving threat environment in Vietnam. One of the early attempts to combat SAMs involved the use of a VQ-1 aircraft operating alongside an A-4 armed with the new US Navy-developed AGM-45 Shrike anti-radiation missile. Lt(jg) Gary Aaron, a Skyhawk pilot with VA-86 deployed in *Independence*, described his experience of attempting to target a SAM site in North Vietnam with the aid of an EA-3B in October 1965 (this mission took place a full two months before the USAF introduced its dedicated anti-SAM 'Wild Weasels' into theatre);

'I was scheduled one day when the overcast started at about 3000 ft and topped out at above 25,000 ft. The "Peter Rabbit" [VQ-1 EA-3B] was to fly a track along the coast of North Vietnam and I was to tuck in real close for radar signature reasons. The climb out was eventful in that I had to keep saying "gimme one" [asking the A-3 pilot to slightly reduce power because he was pulling away from the Skyhawk]. Those two J57s were pretty powerful. The whole idea was that I was to fly tucked in on the sea side of the EA-3 and we would gradually work our way closer and closer to the beach while they sorted out the signals and looked for a SAM site for me to shoot. I actually flew wing on the engine nacelle because the jet's wingtip flopped like a Bluegill [fish] on a small hook.

'The idea was that the EA-3B would listen, as would I, to the PRF [pulse repetition frequency of the SA-2's "Fan Song" target-tracking radar]. If we got the dreaded "warble" I was to take the "Whale's" directions for heading, lock-on and then shoot a Shrike at the site.

'Did I mention we were "Popeye" [completely in the clouds] all the time? Finally, we got a good signal and the EA-3B called "270", which meant I was to break away and head 270 degrees [due west], get a target lock-on, push over and fire at the system's indication. I did all of that and then called "Fox" when the missile was headed down range. The EA-3 crew told me later that 51 seconds after I'd launched the "Fan Song" went down. Did I get it? Who knows?'

VQ-1 quietly, and professionally, carried out its critical work throughout the duration of the war in Southeast Asia. Befitting its decidedly low-key modus operandi, the squadron's contribution to combat operations in Vietnam is only rarely acknowledged. This was directly related to its work at high classification levels that did not lend itself to public release. The squadron received three Navy Unit Commendation Medals for its effort, the citation for one of them speaking volumes when it said '(VQ-1) has been directly instrumental in saving countless lives of US air combat pilots and crewmen over North Vietnam'.

'HEAVY PHOTO'

The US Navy procured 30 A3D-2P photo-reconnaissance Skywarriors in the late 1950s, these jets subsequently becoming RA-3Bs in 1962. The aircraft had a small, pressurised compartment aft of the flightdeck that housed a battery of high-resolution cameras. Behind that were small bays for photo-flash bombs, which would be used to produce light for night photography. As with conventional A3Ds, the aircraft was flown by a crew of three.

The A3D-2Ps were dispersed to the US Navy's two 'Heavy Photo' squadrons, VAP-61 and VAP-62, located at Guam and Jacksonville, respectively. Both units provided detachments as AirPac and AirLant required for high quality photography, with dets working off the beach or from carriers. In performing this specialised role they complemented the better known 'Light Photo' (VFP) squadrons, which flew photo-configured Cougars, and Crusaders during the same period.

Among the most notable work done by VAP was cartographic support, where photographs taken by A3D-2Ps were used to develop new maps and charts of previously under-documented areas such as Alaska, Australia and Southeast Asia.

When the Vietnam War started VAP-61 was based at Guam with ten RA-3Bs. With the initiation of combat operations it immediately went to work off Seventh Fleet carriers to provide photographic and cartographic support for strike planning. In many cases the tasking would be performed by a single aircraft that lived a nomadic life where it would launch off one carrier and recover at the end of the mission onboard a different vessel. In 1965 detachments at Da Nang and Don Muang (near Bangkok, in Thailand) supported the squadron's widespread operations, with RA-3Bs also using Cubi Point extensively.

Starting in August 1966, VAP-61 was tasked with taking infrared (IR) photography of the Ho Chi Minh Trail at night in order to locate supply and camp areas. The IR missions required the RA-3B to fly at about 1500 ft above the terrain at 350 knots, which, not surprisingly, made them

The RA-3B was noted for its photo compartment immediately forward of the wing that contained a battery of high-resolution cameras – the ports through which these took photographs can be seen on the underside of this jet. Indeed, they are all open. Immediately aft of the cameras are the two photo-flash bomb-bays (*US Navy*)

A classic 'hero picture' of an RA-3B crew prior to the start of the Vietnam War. This trio were serving with VAP-62 at NAS Jacksonville at the time, and they represent the typical Heavy Photo crew that would soon take their aircraft into combat. The men are identified as, from left to right, Lts Herb Nichols and Rod Jenkins and PH1 Jack Carter (*US Navy*)

a ripe target for AAA. The undulating terrain was also a concern, with more than one crew reporting that it had been shot at from ridgelines *above* the aircraft, and at least one photo-jet returning home with foliage embedded in the wings.

Concerned about the lack of camouflage the standard US Navy paint scheme provided RA-3Bs when flying such missions, a detachment OinC had his men buy every can of black spray paint they could find at the Cubi Point Exchange. He then had one, or more, RA-3Bs re-sprayed in an overall dull black scheme. The results were deemed to be excellent, giving crews at least some relief as they continued their low altitude night work over the trail. Other aircraft followed, reportedly being repainted by aerospace contractor NIPPI in Japan. Perhaps unsurprisingly, the bureaucratic US Navy had other ideas and the squadron soon received a

VAP-61 was based at Agana, on Guam, and provided detachments throughout Southeast Asia during the war. RA-3B BuNo 144835/SS 912 is shown here flying off Pati Point and Andersen AFB, on Guam, during the early 1960s. The single porthole was a quick recognition feature for this variant. BuNo 144835 failed to return from a night reconnaissance mission over North Vietnam on 25 August 1967, its three-man crew being listed as killed in action (*US Navy*)

By 1967 VAP-61 realised that its low-altitude night missions over North Vietnam required some form of camouflage in order to reduce the risk RA-3B crews were facing from groundfire. The squadron came up with an overall black scheme that was applied to a number of its jets. This shot, taken on *Constellation* during the 1967 cruise, shows BuNo 144847 surrounded by CVW-14 aircraft, including a VAH-8 A-3B and VQ-1 EA-3B. SS 910 would be lost on a mission off *Oriskany* with its three crew on 1 January 1968 (*Rich Dann Collection*)

'cease and desist' order from Naval Air Systems Command. It was told that the impromptu (and apparently effective) black paint scheme was not authorized, and the unit would have to wait for a special camouflage scheme that was being developed by the NARF at Alameda.

What VAP-61 got was a complex, mottled three-tone grey scheme applied to aircraft that were fresh from being overhauled by NARF – similar camouflage was also applied to the AP-2H Neptunes of VAH-21. The squadron's general conclusion was that the grey spotted paint was not as effective as their black, field-applied effort, particularly when the gunners were on ridgelines shooting down at them. Nonetheless, this became the standard camouflage scheme for the rest of the war.

The squadron's hazardous missions led to at least four aircraft returning with AAA damage, with one crewman reported as wounded. It also lost a quartet of RA-3Bs – the highest attrition rate suffered by any of the 'Whale' squadrons during the war. The first aircraft destroyed was

During 1968 the NARF depot at Alameda repainted a number of RA-3Bs in this three-tone grey camouflage for VAP-61. BuNo 144831 sits in fresh paint at California in May of that year, its photo-flash bomb-bay doors open and pinned with red flags (*Bill Swisher via Rich Dann*)

In this photograph taken at Agana in the late 1960s, a typical RA-3B crew – photo-technician/gunner PH1c R Laurie, photo-navigator/assistant pilot Lt(jg) D Schwikert and pilot Lt Cdr Chas D Litford – pose with BuNo 144846. In front of the aircraft are the various camera systems that could be carried by the jet. The photo technician could change film magazines, adjust apertures, correct malfunctions and rearrange cameras by accessing the pressurised camera compartment in flight. Placed in storage at MASDC for a number of years after the Vietnam War, BuNo 144846 was retrieved in 1982 and sent to NARF Alameda to be converted into an ERA-3B. It was subsequently assigned to VAQ-34 the following year. Eventually stricken, the jet was acquired by Hughes for spare parts reclamation for its fleet of civilian-registered A-3s. The remains of the aircraft were cut up for scrap in 1999 after the removal of all usable components (*US Navy*)

BuNo 144842/SS 907 on the night of 13 June 1966. Flying from *Hancock*, it crashed near the mouth of the Gia Hoi River, killing Lt Cdr John Glanville, Lt(jg) George Gierak and PHC Bennie Lambton. The second RA-3B loss came on 25 August 1967 when BuNo 144835/SS 901 (which had been damaged during a night mission some ten days earlier, losing 3000 lbs of fuel from a punctured wing tank) failed to return from a night reconnaissance mission. The crew was on temporary duty from VAP-62, Cdr Ed Jacobs, Lt(jg) Jim Zavocky and ADJ2 Ron Bois-Clair all being listed as killed in action.

Roughly six weeks later, on 14 October, BuNo 144844 was hit by AAA south of Thanh Hoa while conducting a day reconnaissance event along the North Vietnamese coastline. The crew bailed out and the aircraft hit the water about ten miles offshore. While Lt(jg) M M Moser and ADJ2 Jim Shaw were recovered by a US Navy 'Big Mother' H-3, pilot Lt Cdr Rob Vaughn was lost.

VAP-61's final combat loss occurred on 1 January 1968 when BuNo 144847/SS 910 was hit by AAA during a mission off *Oriskany*. The aircraft is believed to have crashed into the sea about 30 miles off Dong Hoi, killing Cdr Dick Dennison, Lt(jg) Terrence Hanley and PHCS Henry Herrin. It would be the last combat-related A-3 loss of the war. Two other RA-3Bs would be lost in-theatre due to operational mishaps, BuNo 144828 on 16 June 1967 following a fire during a test flight from Cubi Point and BuNo 144826 on 8 August 1969 when its engines flamed out because of fuel flow problems whilst on a logistics flight from Da Nang.

VAP-61 ceased operations over Vietnam on 31 January 1970, its aircraft returning to Guam. From here they continued to provide support to the Pacific Fleet by photo-mapping locations such as Diego Garcia and remote parts of Alaska. The squadron was disestablished on 1 July 1971, with its aircraft being taken over by VQ-1.

BOMBARDIER/NAVIGATOR TRAINERS

Rounding out the 'Whale' variants were 12 A3D-2Ts built in 1959-60 as bombardier/navigator trainers, with five student seats in the aft cabin

and provisions for wing pylons to carry practice bomb dispensers. Contrary to several references, none were built, or ever retrofitted, with dual flight controls. They were also the only A-3s constructed with the third seat facing forward (due to the lack of tail guns), and all were built with CLE wings.

Re-designated TA-3Bs in 1962, the 'T-birds' would eventually be used for pilot training in the RAGs and as squadron hacks within the VQ community. One, BuNo 144865, would be completely refitted, and re-designated as an EA-3B in the mid-1980s when there was a shortage of such airframes. The TA series became the last of the entire Skywarrior family to operate off a flightdeck while conducting carrier qualifications with VAQ-33 in 1989.

Up to five TA-3Bs were re-configured as VIP transports during their lives by the NARF depot at Alameda, these aircraft boasting more comfortable seats, panelling and a toilet. Official documents indicate

The groundcrewman gives the 'Hold brakes' signal to the pilot of a VAP-61 RA-3B as it returns from a sortie, as evidenced by the open drag chute door at the rear of the aircraft. BuNo 146446/SS 90 is in standard pre-war paint. It was also one of only two of its type to be built with CLE wings, both of which would be rebuilt post-war into ERA-3Bs for VAQ-33 (*US Navy via Rich Dann*)

The one and only true VA-3B, BuNo 142672 sits at North Island in the mid 1960s with a two-star flag flying from its upper hatch. It carries a Department of the Navy logo on its tail, being assigned to a special logistics detachment out of NAF Washington, D.C.. Five TA-3Bs were modified with VIP interiors for a similar role, but they were apparently never formally re-designated as 'VAs' (*Bill Swisher via Tailhook Association*)

'Ashes to Ashes' – the hulk of TA-3B BuNo 144864 going through SARDIP at Alameda in January 1981. A VIP-configured 'Whale', the aircraft was accepted in March 1960 and stricken in February 1977 (*Author*)

that they retained their TA-3B designation throughout their lives, however, in spite of their special interiors. To quote one pilot familiar with the issue 'the Navy didn't want the Air Force or Congress to know we had that many VIP aircraft. The USAF thought it was their mission and Congressmen ask too many questions'. The one true VA-3B was EA-3B BuNo 142672 that was converted at the Norfolk NARF depot. After several years of duty flying from Washington, D.C., it was placed in storage within MASDC in Arizona in 1974. Here it languished until 1980, when it was retrieved from the 'boneyard' and sent to Alameda for overhaul prior to being returned to the fleet. BuNo 142672 was provided with a more spartan six-seat back end for use as an admin support aircraft by VQ-1 as its PR 111.

Typically, one or two of the VIP-configured TA-3Bs worked out of Naval Air Facility Washington with either VR-1 or a special logistics det that supported US Navy headquarters. They gave the Chief of Naval Operations (CNO) and US Navy staff officers the opportunity to fly out to a carrier if necessary, although this requirement was greatly reduced by the 1980s. The TA-3Bs also provided a comfortable aircraft that could fly coast-to-coast unrefuelled at more than 0.8 Mach – something their Department of Defense, USAF and US Army counterparts could not do in a C-140 JetStar or T-39 Sabreliner.

Two TA-3Bs were destroyed in mishaps, RVAH-3 losing BuNo 144861 after an engine fire on takeoff from NAS Albany, Georgia, on 27 August 1973, with the crew bailing out, and VQ-2 VIP-configured BuNo 144863 crashing on departure from Naples with eight men onboard on 9 July 1974 – no one survived the latter accident. VA-3B BuNo 142672 would be lost off Guam with VQ-1 on 23 January 1985, resulting in the deaths of all nine crew, including the squadron commanding officer, Cdr John T Mitchell. It is believed that the aircraft probably suffered dual ATM failure, rendering the jet uncontrollable.

TIMELESS 'WHALE'

With the removal of the EKA-3B from the fleet in 1974 the future of the 'Whale' was certainly open to question. Within the US Navy many assumed that the A-3's end was near and that the Skywarrior only had a few more years to go before it would be retired. This was certainly the case in the USAF, where the 'Whale's' distant cousin, the EB-66, had been 'put down' by the end of 1974. What practically nobody foresaw, however, was that the 'Whale' was far from extinct. Indeed, it still had another 17 years to go in uniform alone.

As of January 1974 there were still 95 A-3s of all varieties in the inventory. With VAQ-130 having moved from California to Whidbey for Prowler conversion, the A-3 replacement training role was assigned to Naval Air Reserve Unit (NARU) Alameda, which soon had three TA-3Bs and an RA-3B assigned to carry out its new duties. With three regular squadrons to train (VQ-1, VQ-2 and VAQ-33) as well as two reserve tanker units, NARU was neither staffed nor equipped to handle a continuous throughput of students, so the fleet replacement squadron (FRS) tasking was transferred to VAQ-33 at NAS Norfolk, Virginia, in October 1977.

VAQ-33 had been the final fleet operator of the A-1 Skyraider in the US Navy, retiring its last EA-1F 'Queer Spads' in 1970. The squadron was soon adopted by the newly established FEWSG to provide realistic EW training for the fleet. The 'Firebirds', as VAQ-33 was now nicknamed, became a composite EW unit with a mixed force of EA-4s, EF-4s, NC-121s and A-3s, all being specially configured with jamming and chaff systems. The squadron's first jamming 'Whales' were a pair

VAQ-33 became the A-3 RAG in 1977, receiving five TA-3Bs to train pilots and crew. BuNo 144858/GD 25 is shown here in the pattern at NAS Key West on 10 February 1981, with the author 'driving' (*Lindsay Peacock*)

BuNo 146447/GD 4, which was one of VAQ-33's quartet of ERA-3Bs, prepares for a mission at NAS Roosevelt Roads on 14 October 1981. It carries ALQ-76 pods on the wings and shows the fuselage-mounted ram air turbines installed to power the internal ALT-27 jamming system. In February 1972 this aircraft was hit by an AIM-7 Sparrow air-to-air missile fired by a Royal Navy Phantom FG 1 operating off HMS *Ark Royal* (RO 9). The crew managed to land back at 'Rosey Roads' minus one engine. Retired in May 1990, this aircraft was shredded at the Aircraft Maintenance And Regeneration Center in July 2012 (*Author*)

of converted bombers, closely followed by four ex-Heavy Photo RA-3Bs that were extensively modified into ERA-3B configuration through the fitment of internal jammers (ALT-27 and DLQ-3) and ALQ-76 external pods, as well as an ALE-2 bulk chaff dispenser. The area previously occupied by the photographic equipment was converted into a crew station for an EWO, along with an additional seat for an observer or trainee.

The ERA-3B 'Warbirds', as they were called within the unit, weighed 50,000 lbs empty, which precluded them from going to the carrier – they would be land-based throughout their careers. The EW training mission could be hazardous at times. For example, in February 1972 BuNo 146447/GD 4 was hit by an AIM-7 Sparrow air-to-air missile fired by a Royal Navy Phantom FG 1 operating off HMS *Ark Royal* (RO 9). Luckily the weapon had a telemetry head fitted, rather than a warhead, although it did remove the starboard engine from the 'Whale'. The crew was highly experienced, being made up of squadron CO, Cdr Lou Hettinger, and B/N Lt Cdr Jim Vambell, and they were able to recover the heavily damaged aircraft at nearby NAS Roosevelt Roads, Puerto Rico.

In order to carry out the FRS tasking, VAQ-33 established a training department with five TA-3Bs at NAS Norfolk, before moving to nearby Oceana, and its longer runways, in 1978. The squadron subsequently transferred to NAS Key West, Florida, in 1980 and continued to operate from here as the last of five A-3 training squadrons to have served with the US Navy.

In 1982-83 another quartet of RA-3Bs were pulled out of the 'boneyard' and modified into ERA-3Bs with the fitting of an ALT-40 jamming system and ALE-43 chaff dispensers. The 'new' airframes were used to establish NAS Point Mugu-based VAQ-34 in March 1983 as FEWSG's second squadron (supporting Pacific Fleet assets), with VAQ-33's aircraft being modified with this new equipment as well. One ERA-3B was lost on 11 January 1987 when VAQ-33's BuNo

144827/GD 101 had a mid-air collision with a squadron KA-3B off Alaska. The tanker, with the squadron's CO in the pilot's seat, was able to land at Elmendorf AFB on a single engine. The 'Warbird', however, went into the Pacific Ocean with its pilot and EWO. The navigator and plane captain bailed out and were rescued.

By late 1987 the 'Whale' population was down to 44 A-3s of all flavours still flying. Operators included VQ-1 and -2, continuing with national-level surveillance missions off the beach with EA-3Bs, and VAQ-33 and -34 with their ERA-3Bs, TA-3Bs and two tankers. The Reserves also continued to fly A-3s from Alameda, while test and evaluation units had a handful of modified jets at China Lake and Point Mugu.

At this point the end for the A-3 in US Navy service was only four years away. There was growing concern within the Naval Aviation community as to the safety of the aircraft due to a continuing string of accidents since the end of the Vietnam War. While the number of jets involved (ten) was significant in itself, it was the loss of 43 men during this period that was considered most alarming. The deaths of seven crew in the crash of an EA-3B during a night recovery onboard USS *Nimitz* (CVN-68) in the Mediterranean rapidly solidified the effort to get the 'Whale' off the boat.

FEWSG operated eight ERA-3Bs, which were photo-birds modified for land-based electronic warfare training with VAQ-33 and VAQ-34. This section of VAQ-34 'Warbirds' was involved in a 'Hey Rube' fighter EW event off San Diego on 14 July 1986 (*Author*)

The inherent versatility of the A-3 airframe led to it being used for many years as a developmental aircraft, working for both US Navy and industry contractors through to 2011. NAS Point Mugu, California, was home for most of the US Navy's test 'Whales', like NRA-3B BuNo 144825 of the Pacific Missile Test Center. It is seen here with its 'Snoopy' nose in 1982, along with what appears to be a chaff pod. It would end up being flown to Whidbey Island on 29 April 2011 so that it could be put on display as part of the Naval Air Station's memorial to fallen personnel (*Michael Grove*)

Although VQ-1 and VQ-2 pulled their EA-3Bs off the carriers during 1987, they would continue to provide national-level electronic surveillance from the beach until September 1991. Indeed, VQ-2 had flown the aircraft in combat as part of Operation *Desert Storm* during the first three months of that year. This EA-3B, 'Ranger 18' (BuNo 144852), is from VQ-2 and it is shown onboard *John F Kennedy* in December 1980 (*Lindsay Peacock*)

On the evening of 25 January 1987 'Ranger 12' (BuNo 144850) launched on a surveillance mission with a full crew of seven. Following several unsuccessful approaches at the back of the ship the 'Whale' was sent to the duty A-7 tanker for more fuel. The Corsair II's package proved to be 'sour', or unusable. Faced with the prospect of having the crew bail out into the winter waters at night, the ship decided to rig the barricade. The final pass was like all of the others – high all the way in and the pilot did not quickly cut (shut-off) the engines as required over the ramp. The A-3 floated over the wires and impacted the top strap of the barricade (which was also mis-rigged, as it lacked a critical piece of gear to properly tighten the upper strap) with the nose gear. The aircraft duly flew through the barricade and went over the angle, where it impacted the water. The rescue helicopter was quickly overhead and noted no movement inside the aircraft, which temporarily floated on the surface of the water. All seven men went down with the EA-3B when it sank a few minutes later.

This accident was followed on the night of 26 June by the crash of VQ-1 EA-3B BuNo 144854 while conducting carrier landing practice at NAS Miramar, California. All three onboard perished. After consideration of both mishaps, and another incident where a VQ-2 jet trapped with a failed nose gear, orders went out to halt A-3 carrier deployments. Both VQ-1 and VQ-2 had removed their aircraft from carrier duty by the end of 1987, although they retained them for use from the beach. The FRS within VAQ-33 continued to day qualify carrier instructors for proficiency reasons for another two years, however. The last 'Whale' trap and cat took place in August 1989 off the Atlantic coast.

The final crash involving an A-3 occurred on 13 January 1988 when VAK-208 KA-3B BuNo 147665 impacted Pyramid Lake northeast of Reno, Nevada, while flying in the late afternoon on a low-level mission. All three crew onboard were killed. It was the last of more than 100 Skywarriors destroyed in crashes – a toll that accounted for a staggering 42 per cent of production. In at least 20 other cases A-3s were stricken following in-flight incidents or gear-up landings. Nonetheless, within the 'Whale' community it was frequently said, only half-jokingly, that the reason the aircraft had lasted so long was the fact that it *didn't* have ejection seats!

Yet even with the end finally in sight for the mighty 'Whale', VQ-2 sent the Skywarrior into combat yet again when it deployed a pair of EA-3Bs to Jeddah, in Saudi Arabia, in late 1990 for what became Operation *Desert Storm*. The aircraft provided the same service they had long supplied the fleet – expert electronic surveillance in a combat environment, providing pre- and post-strike reconnaissance for the Red Sea carrier battlegroups. Indeed, a single EA-3B was on station for each

EA-3B BuNo 146457/NF 005 of VQ-1 Det A sits on the ramp outside the Alameda depot in June 1985. The jet carries *USS Midway* titling and an NF tail code following its assignment to CVW-5, along with BuNo 144854/NF 010. The latter aircraft crashed on the night of 26 June 1987 while conducting carrier landing practice at NAS Miramar, California. All three onboard perished (*Michael Grove*)

VQ-2's 'Ranger 16' prepares to land aboard *Kitty Hawk* in the Pacific on 3 February 1987, CV-63 having just commenced a WestPac/World Cruise with CVW-9 embarked. The vessel embarked a single jet from both VQ-1 and VQ-2 for the deployment (*US Navy*)

On 30 April 2009 EA-3B BuNo 146457 'Ranger 007' was craned onboard USS *Wasp* (LHD-1) for transportation back to the USA from Naval Station (NAVSTA) Rota, Spain. This marked the first time in more than 20 years that a 'Whale' was chocked and chained to the flightdeck of an active US Navy warship. In July 2007 the then CO of NAVSTA Rota notified the A-3 Skywarrior Association that because of long-term plans for the installation, the EA-3 presently located on display outside the Rota BOQ would need to be relocated to the USA or end up being scrapped. The association duly instigated a 'Save the Whale' campaign, and through the efforts and contributions of individuals and corporations 'Ranger 007' was shipped to the USA and eventually placed on display onboard the carrier *Yorktown* within the Patriots Point Museum in Mount Pleasant, South Carolina (*US Navy*)

carrier strike into Iraq, the 'Whale' crews coordinating their activities with E-2Cs and EA-6Bs for the targeting of HARM against Iraqi SAM and radar sites. EA-3Bs also provided a similar service to USAF elements attacking targets in northern Iraq, the 'Whales' flying from Naval Support Activity Souda Bay, Crete.

With the end of combat in Iraq, VQ-2 wrapped up its jet operations and sent its few remaining aircraft back to the US. The A-3's retirement from active duty occurred at NAS Key West on 27 September 1991 when the CO of VAQ-33, Cdr Bruce 'Chicken Lips' Nottke, presided over a formal ceremony celebrating more than 35 years of Skywarrior operations by the US Navy. The event was attended by Capt Paul Stevens, the first CO of VAH-1 in 1956, as well as former A-3 navigator Vice Admiral Dick Dunleavy, at that time the head of US Naval Aviation as OP-05. Also present was retired Capt James 'Pac Man' Vambell, the legendary former commander of FEWSG and VAQ-33 who led all others with the most flight time in the A-3 – more than 6500 hours in type.

Even that would not be the end of the A-3, however, as the aircraft would continue to be used by defence contractors for a further two decades. Thunderbird Aviation at Phoenix, Arizona, and Hughes (later Raytheon) had a weird and wonderful assortment of modified A-3s operating as electronics test beds out of Van Nuys, California, until 30 June 2011. On that date the last flight of an A-3 Skywarrior was made by Raytheon's chief pilot, Ron 'Coyote' Woltman, Cdr US Navy (Ret), when he delivered EA-3B N875RS (BuNo 144865) to Pensacola for display. When he shut down the J57 engines at the end of the flight the distinctive howl – the song of the 'Whale' – passed into history.

APPENDICES

APPENDIX A

A-3 SKYWARRIOR FAMILY

Bombers

A3D-1/A-3A	(49 built)	modified as A3D-1Q (EA-3A) (5) and A3D-1P/NRA-3A (NA-3A)
A3D-2/A-3B	(163 built)	modified as KA-3B (85), EKA-3B* (39) and NA-3B

* Many EKA-3Bs returned to KA-3B configuration by 1975

Versions

A3D-2T/TA-3B*	(12 built)	modified as EA-3B (1) and NTA-3B (1)
A3D-2Q/EA-3B	(24 built)	modified as VA-3B (1)
A3D-2P/RA-3B	(30 built)	modified as NRA-3B, ERA-3B (8) and UA-3B (1)

* Five TA-3Bs had VIP interiors installed by NARF at Alameda but retained TA-3B designation. At this time it appears as if only BuNo 142672 was formally designated as a VA-3B

APPENDIX B

A-3 SQUADRONS OF THE VIETNAM WAR

NAS Whidbey Island

VAH-2 'Royal Rampants'	A-3B and KA-3B
VAH-4 'Four-Runners'	A-3B and KA-3B
VAH-8 'Fireballers'	A-3B and KA-3B
VAH-10/VAQ-129 'Vikings'	A-3B, KA-3B and EKA-3B
VAH-123 'Professionals'	A-3A, A-3B, KA-3B and TA-3B (RAG)

NAS Alameda

VAW-13 'Zappers'	EKA-3B
VAQ-130 'Zappers'	EKA-3B, KA-3B and TA-3B (RAG 1971-74)
VAQ-131 'Holly Greens'	EKA-3B and KA-3B
VAQ-132 'Scorpions'	EKA-3B and KA-3B
VAQ-133 'Golden Zappers'	EKA-3B and KA-3B
VAQ-134 'Garudas'	EKA-3B and KA-3B
VAQ-135 'Homebrew'	EKA-3B and KA-3B
VAQ-208 'Jockeys'	KA-3B (Reserves)
VAQ-308 'Griffins'	KA-3B (Reserves)

Special Mission

VQ-1 'World Watchers'	EA-3B, TA-3B, RA-3B, VA-3B and A-3B (with support from Rota-based VQ-2)
VAP-61 'World Recorders'	RA-3B and A-3B (with support from Jacksonville-based VAP-62)

APPENDIX C

A-3B, KA-3B AND EKA-3B DEPLOYMENTS OF THE VIETNAM WAR

1-11/64	Bon Homme Richard/CVW-19	VAH-4 Det E (ZB)	3 A-3Bs
4-12/64	Ticonderoga/CVW-5	VAH-4 Det B (ZB)	3 A-3Bs
5/64-2/65	Constellation/CVW-14	VAH-10 (NK 100)	12 A-3Bs
8/64-5/65	Ranger/CVW-9	VAH-2 Det M (NL/NG 800)	3 A-3Bs
10/64-5/65	Hancock/CVW-21	VAH-4 Det L (ZB)	3 A-3Bs
12/64-11/65	Coral Sea/CVW-15	VAH-2 (NL 600)	9 A-3Bs
3-11/65	Midway/CVW-2	VAH-8 (NE 690)	8 A-3Bs
5-12/65	Independence/CVW-7	VAH-4 Det 62 (AG 810)	3 A-3Bs
4-12/65	Oriskany/CVW-16	VAH-4 Det G (ZB)	3 A-3Bs
9/65-5/66	Ticonderoga/CVW-5	VAH-4 Det B (ZB)	3 A-3Bs
10/65-6/66	Kitty Hawk/CVW-11	VAH-4 Det C (ZB)	3 A-3Bs
10/65-6/66	Enterprise/CVW-9	VAH-4 Det M (ZB 110)	3 A-3Bs
12/65-8/66	Ranger/CVW-14	VAH-2 Det F (NL 830)	3 A-3Bs
1-7/66	NAS Cubi Point/(none)	VAH-4 Det Y (ZB 000)	2 A-3Bs
5-11/66	Oriskany/CVW-16	VAH-4 Det G (ZB)	3 A-3Bs

5-12/66	*Constellation*/CVW-15	VAH-8 (NL 600)	5 A-3Bs
6/66-2/67	*Franklin D Roosevelt*/CVW-1	VAH-10 Det 42 (AB 600)	4 A-3Bs
7/66-2/67	*Coral Sea*/CVW-2	VAH-2 Det A (ZA 690)	5 A-3Bs
10/66-5/67	*Ticonderoga*/CVW-19	VAH-4 Det E (ZB 890)	3 A-3Bs
11/66-6/67	*Kitty Hawk*/CVW-11	VAH-4 Det C/63 (ZB)	5 A-3Bs
11/66-7/67	*Enterprise*/CVW-9	VAH-2 Det M/65 (ZA 110)	5 A-3Bs
1-7/67	*Hancock*/CVW-5	VAH-4 Det B/19 (ZB)	3 A-3Bs
1-8/67	*Bon Homme Richard*/CVW-21	VAH-4 Det L/31 (ZB 890)	3 A-3Bs
5-12/67	*Constellation*/CVW-14	VAH-8 Det 64 (NK 100)	5 KA-3Bs
6/67-1/68	*Oriskany*/CVW-16	VAH-4 Det G/34 (AH 610)	3 KA-3Bs
6-8/67	*Forrestal*/CVW-17	VAH-10 Det 59 (AA 610)	3 KA-3Bs
6/67-4/68	*Coral Sea*/CVW-15	VAH-2 Det D (NL 600)	3 KA-3Bs
11/67-5/68	*Ranger*/CVW-2	VAH-2 Det 61 (ZA 600)	2 KA-3Bs
11/67-5/68	*Ranger*/CVW-2	VAW-13 Det 61 (VR 720)	3 EKA-3Bs
11/67-6/68	*Kitty Hawk*/CVW-11	VAH-4 Det 63 (ZB)	5 KA-3Bs
12/67-8/68	*Ticonderoga*/CVW-19	VAH-4 Det 14 (ZB)	3 KA-3Bs
1-7/68	*Enterprise*/CVW-9	VAH-2 Det 65 (ZA)	3 KA-3Bs
1-7/68	*Enterprise*/CVW-9	VAW-13 Det 65 (VR 720)	2 KA-3Bs
1-10/68	*Bon Homme Richard*/CVW-5	VAW-13 Det 31 (NF 030)	3 EKA-3Bs
4-12/68	*America*/CVW-6	VAH-10 Det 66 (AE 010)	2 KA-3Bs
4-10/68	*America*/CVW-6	VAW-13 Det 66 (AE 710)	3 EKA-3Bs
10-12/68	*America*/CVW-6	VAQ-130 Det 66 (AE 710)	3 EKA-3Bs
5-11/68	*Constellation*/CVW-14	VAH-2 Det 64 (NK 100)	2 KA-3Bs
11/68-1/69	*Constellation*/CVW-14	VAH-10 Det 64 (NK 100)	2 KA-3Bs
5-10/68	*Constellation*/CVW-14	VAW-13 Det 64 (NK 110)	3 EKA-3Bs
10/68-1/69	*Constellation*/CVW-14	VAQ-130 Det 64 (NK 110)	3 EKA-3Bs
7-10/68	*Hancock*/CVW-21	VAW-13 Det 19 (NP 020)	3 EKA-3Bs
10/68-3/69	*Hancock*/CVW-21	VAQ-130 Det 19 (NP 020)	3 EKA-3Bs
9-10/68	*Coral Sea*/CVW-15	VAH-2 Det 43 (NL 700)	2 KA-3Bs
10/68-4/69	*Coral Sea*/CVW-15	VAH-10 Det 43 (NL 700)	2 KA-3Bs
9-10/68	*Coral Sea*/CVW-15	VAW-13 Det 43 (VR 010)	3 EKA-3Bs
10/68-4/69	*Coral Sea*/CVW-15	VAQ-130 Det 43 (VR 010)	3 EKA-3Bs
10/68-5/69	*Ranger*/CVW-2	VAH-10 Det 61 (NE 610)	2 KA-3Bs
10/68-5/69	*Ranger*/CVW-2	VAQ-130 Det 61 (NE 612)	3 EKA-3Bs
12/68-8/69	*Kitty Hawk*/CVW-11	VAQ-131 (NH 610)	3 EKA-3Bs/2 KA-3Bs
1-10/69	*Bon Homme Richard*/CVW-5	VAQ-130 Det 31 (NF 610)	3 EKA-3Bs
1-10/69	*Enterprise*/CVW-9	VAQ-132 (NG 610)	3 EKA-3Bs/2 KA-3Bs
2-9/69	*Ticonderoga*/CVW-16	VAQ-130 Det 14 (AH 610)	3 EKA-3Bs
4-10/69	*Oriskany*/CVW-19	VAQ-130 Det 34 (NM 610)	3 EKA-3Bs
8/69-4/70	*Hancock*/CVW-21	VAH-10 Det 19 (NP 610)	3 KA-3Bs
8/69-5/70	*Constellation*/CVW-14	VAQ-133 (NK 610)	3 EKA-3Bs/2 KA-3Bs
9/69-7/70	*Coral Sea*/CVW-15	VAQ-135 (NL 610)	3 EKA-3Bs/1 KA-3B
10/69-6/70	*Ranger*/CVW-2	VAQ-134 (NE 610)	3 EKA-3Bs/2 KA-3Bs
3-9/70	*Shangri-La*/CVW-8	VAH-10 Det 38 (AJ 610)	3 KA-3Bs
9-12/70	*Shangri-La*/CVW-8	VAQ-129 Det 38 (AJ 610)	3 KA-3Bs
10/70-6/71	*Hancock*/CVW-21	VAQ-129 (NP 610)	3 EKA-3Bs
4-11/70	*Bon Homme Richard*/CVW-5	VAQ-130 Det 31 (NF 610)	3 EKA-3Bs
4-12/70	*America*/CVW-9	VAQ-132 (NG 610)	3 EKA-3Bs/2 KA-3Bs
5-12/70	*Oriskany*/CVW-19	VAQ-130 Det 1 (NM 610)	3 EKA-3Bs
11/70-7/71	*Kitty Hawk*/CVW-11	VAQ-133 (NH 610)	3 EKA-3Bs/2 KA-3Bs
12/70-6/71	*Ranger*/CVW-2	VAQ-134 (NE 610)	3 EKA-3Bs/2 KA-3Bs
4-11/71	*Midway*/CVW-5	VAQ-130 Det 2 (NF 610)	3 EKA-3Bs
5-12/71	*Oriskany*/CVW-19	VAQ-130 Det 3 (NM 610)	3 EKA-3Bs
6/71-2/72	*Enterprise*/CVW-14	VAQ-130 Det 4 (NK 610)	3 EKA-3Bs
10/71-6/72	*Constellation*/CVW-9	VAQ-130 Det 1 (NG 610)	3 EKA-3Bs
11/71-6/72	*Coral Sea*/CVW-15	VAQ-135 Det 3 (NL 610)	3 EKA-3Bs
1-10/72	*Hancock*/CVW-21	VAQ-135 Det 5 (NP 610)	3 EKA-3Bs
2-11/72	*Kitty Hawk*/CVW-11	VAQ-135 Det 1 (NH 610)	3 EKA-3Bs
4/72-3/73	*Midway*/CVW-5	VAQ-130 Det 2 (NF 610)	3 EKA-3Bs
11/72-6/73	*Ranger*/CVW-2	VAQ-130 Det 4 (NE 610)	3 EKA-3Bs
3-8/73	*Coral Sea*/CVW-15	VAQ-135 Det 3 (NL 610)	3 EKA-3Bs
8-11/73	*Coral Sea*/CVW-15	VAQ-130 Det 2 (NL 610)	3 EKA-3Bs
5-8/73	*Hancock*/CVW-21	VAQ-135 Det 5 (NL 610)	3 EKA-3Bs
8/73-1/74	*Hancock*/CVW-21	VAQ-130 Det 5 (NL 610)	3 EKA-3Bs

Notes

– AirPac changed detachment letters to numbers in 1968; AirLant used hull numbers throughout.

– KA-3B designation formalised 5/67

APPENDIX D

A-3B BOMB LOADS (1965)

Ordnance	With Tanker Package	Without Tanker Package
500 lb GP (AN-M64)	8	12
1000 lb GP (AN-M65)	3	6
2000 lb GP (AN-M66)	2	4
500 lb (Mk 82)	4	6
1000 lb (Mk 83)	3	4
2000 lb (Mk 84)	0	3
374 lb mine (Mks 50 or 53)	8	12
1000 lb mine (Mks 36 or 52)	3	6
2000 lb mine (Mks 39 or 55)	2	4

Note

– Auxiliary fuel tank, when installed, precluded all ordnance

COLOUR PLATES

Notes on A-3s during the Vietnam War

Fuel vents – A-3s initially had a small fuel system vent that projected from the underside of the port horizontal stabiliser. From BuNo 142650 onward this was replaced in production by a larger and more obvious vent that projected horizontally from the port side of the aft tail section.

Noses and tails – The original A-3 'bomber' nose design was eventually replaced by a 'bobbed' nose that became standard for all A-3Bs and Versions over time. This style appears to have been introduced at the same time as the ASB-7 radar and ALQ-41/51 defensive ECM gear. Eventually almost all A-3Bs, RA-3Bs and EA-3Bs received this nose, although most TA-3Bs retained the 'bomber' style practically to the end of their service lives. Likewise, the original gun turret rear end was replaced during the same period by a more aerodynamic 'dovetail' (or 'duckbutt') design that was intended to hold the rearward-facing ALQ-41/51 gear. This was also retrofitted to practically all bombers and most EA/RA aircraft from the early 1960s. A-3As retained their original noses and tails throughout their lives.

Refuelling probes – These were introduced to A-3Bs in the early 1960s and generally retrofitted throughout the fleet by 1964.

Wings – There were two different wing designs on A-3s, namely 'Basic' and 'Cambered Leading Edge' (CLE). While the wing form was slightly different (to give CLE aircraft a lower landing speed), the quickest way to tell them apart was that Basic had wing slats outboard of the engines only, while CLE also had slats between the engines and fuselage. A total of 67 aircraft were equipped with CLE wings, as were two test aircraft, BuNos 138918 and 138932.

Tanker packages – While all A-3Bs could take refuelling packages by 1964, not all aircraft carried them when the war started. In May 1967 the US Navy formally re-designated jets with the now semi-permanent installation as the KA-3B.

Normal paint – The standard scheme for VAH, VAQ and VQ aircraft throughout the war was gloss light gull grey over insignia white. Application of other markings was left up to the squadron and detachments, the latter frequently devising distinctive deviations from the norm. Maroon was a frequent trim colour for VAQ units as it was the designated shade for their community's 610 series Modex numbers as per Naval Aeronautical Organization Notice (OPNAV) Instruction 3710 (which was also why 100 to 500 series numbers typically used red, yellow, orange, blue and green). There were three known uses of special camouflage on 'Whales' during the Vietnam War. These are covered in the profile notes.

Tailcodes – The US Navy uses a formal Visual Identification System to help distinguish its aircraft. Popularly known as a tailcode, the two-character marking was assigned through the Vietnam period by the Office of the CNO and published annually in the OPNAV 05400. All air wings were given specific tailcodes, which have become well documented over the years. While fighter and attack (VF and VA) squadrons carried the air wing code, many of the 'cat and dog' detachments (typically VAW, VFP and VAH) frequently carried unique codes assigned directly to their squadrons. This was also the case for special mission squadrons like VAP-61 (assigned SS) and VQ-1 (PR).

During the late 1950s Whidbey's squadrons under Hatwing Two were assigned sequential codes starting with 'Z' – VAH-2 (ZA), VAH-4 (ZB), VAH-6 (ZC) and VAH-8 (ZD). These codes were used on deployments by the Whidbey squadrons for several years, even though OPNAV had officially ended their use by VAH-2, -6 and -8 in lieu of air wing codes on 1 July 1959. VAH-4's distinctive ZB code continued to be authorised until the unit's re-designation as VAQ-131 in 1968. VAH-10 was authorised the distinct code ZR for a one-year period in 1969-70.

The 'Zappers' of VAW-13 were assigned the VR code when established in 1959, and the unit retained it through re-designation as VAQ-130 until January 1971, when it was deleted from OPNAV 05400. TR was assigned to VAQWING-13 in 1968 and eventually used by VAQ-130 and -135 between deployments at Alameda. The TR code accompanied the organisation when it moved to Whidbey, being used by VAQ-129 EA-6Bs until the wing was disestablished in July 1972, at which point the Prowler FRS adopted the standard AirPac training squadron code, NJ.

1
A-3B BuNo 147650/NL 601 of VAH-2, USS *Coral Sea* (CVA-43), summer 1965

Working from two carriers in 1964-65, VAH-2 was the first A-3 squadron to deliver ordnance in combat. Two-thirds of the unit (six jets) was deployed in *Coral Sea* with CVW-15, with the remainder (three A-3Bs) joining CVW-8 embarked in *Ranger* as Det Mike. On *Coral Sea* the squadron lost one aircraft (BuNo 147664/NL 604), and NL 601 would be damaged during a landing accident and craned off the ship at some point. Although repaired, BuNo 147650 would itself be destroyed on 6 October 1966 following a mid-air collision with an RVAH-7 RA-5C off southern California. All three men onboard the 'Whale' were killed, while the Vigilante crew ejected safely. NL 601 is shown here with 25 bomb mission marks as well as a 'Battle E' award.

2

A-3B BuNo 147652/ZA 112 of VAH-2 Det M, USS *Enterprise* (CVAN-65), 1966-67

VAH-2 Det Mike deployed five A-3Bs in *Enterprise* with CVW-9 in 1966-67, these aircraft wearing the squadron's distinctive ZA tailcode and using Modex 110 series side numbers. Although ZA 110 is seen here without a tanker package, it does carry an S&H Green Stamps logo on the aft fuselage. These were a popular commercial premium associated with petrol stations and grocery stores in the US where customers would collect stamps and trade them for items in an S&H store. The wry implication here is that VAH-2 gave Green Stamps as part of its refuelling service. Delivered to the US Navy in April 1960, this aircraft became an EKA-3B in November 1967 and was eventually retired to MASDC in August 1973.

3

A-3B BuNo 142662/AG 816 of VAH-4 Det 62, USS *Independence* (CVA-62), 1965

VAH-4 was unique in that it never deployed as a complete squadron, normally supplying three-aircraft detachments to Pacific Fleet modified-*Essex* class carriers. In May 1965 the squadron made its first 'big deck' deployment, providing three A-3Bs as Det 62 to the Atlantic Fleet 'supercarrier' *Independence* for its one and only trip to Vietnam. While most of the detachments wore the squadron's normal ZB tailcode, in this case Det 62's aircraft were adorned with CVW-7's AG markings – something that east coast air wings apparently insisted on. Delivered to the US Navy in April 1959, BuNo 142662 had a long and productive life, being converted into a KA-3B and EKA-3B and later flying with the Alameda Reserves, again as a KA-3B. Retired in 1989, it was scrapped at Alameda as part of the Stricken Aircraft Reclamation Disposal Program (SARDIP).

4

A-3B BuNo 142662/ZB 1 of VAH-4 Det C, USS *Kitty Hawk* (CVA-63), 1965-66

Although *Kitty Hawk's* 1965-66 camouflage trials are well known, a lot of the specific details pertaining to the schemes used remain vague. For example, of the four good photographs the author has seen of VAH-4 Det C's green-painted 'Whale(s)', they all appear to be of the same aircraft but with slightly different markings. A widely published shot of ZB 1 on the ship's flightdeck shows a tailcode and black side number. However, what appear to be later photographs of the same aircraft show it with small white modex and BuNo but no tailcode, as depicted in this profile. It is believed that the paint was applied in Japan, and that the aircraft may have returned home still in green camouflage. BuNo 142662 was on *Independence* prior to *Kitty Hawk*, and the jet appears to have been a cross-deck transfer.

5

A-3B BuNo 138971/ZB 4 of VAH-4 Det 63, USS *Kitty Hawk* (CVA-63), 1967-68

As the A-3's primary role moved to that of a dedicated refuelling aircraft, 'tanker stripes' started appearing on them in order to make it easier for customers to find their assigned refueller in a gaggle of aircraft. VAH-4 led the fleet in use of these markings, with some applications being remarkably dramatic. The number of stripes usually (but not always) matched the last digit of the aircraft's side number, hence the four applied here to ZB 4 – appropriately, the aircraft also carries the name *Tiger* on its nose. Delivered to the US Navy in September 1957, BuNo 138971 lasted as a KA-3B until January 1972, when, like a lot of other veteran naval aircraft, it was retired to MASDC.

6

KA-3B BuNo 142255/ZB 13 of VAH-4 Det 14, USS *Ticonderoga* (CVA-14), 1967-68

For the 1967-68 deployment with 'Tico' VAH-4 Det 14 carried a variation on the tanker stripe theme, with this example being marked with a pair of thin blue stripes that were repeated chordwise on top of the wings outboard of the engines. This would be Heavy Four's last deployment to Vietnam, as it returned to Whidbey in August 1968 and was re-designated as VAQ-131 on 1 November. Accepted by the US Navy in February 1958, BuNo 142255 would be converted into an EKA-3B in 1968 and then sent to MASDC for storage in May 1975.

7

A-3B BuNo 147667/NE 695 of VAH-8, USS *Midway* (CVA-41), 1965

The 'Fireballers' of Heavy Eight made three deployments to Vietnam, always as a complete squadron. The first cruise was with CVW-2 in *Midway*, the unit embarking eight A-3Bs. NE 695 shows two bomb markings and five stylised gas pumps, each with the number '5' (apparently referring to five aircraft saves each), on its forward fuselage. The jet also has a very small version of the Mobil gas Pegasus logo, complete with *Go Mobil* titling, beneath the aft canopy section. BuNo 147667 was the next-to-last A-3 built, being converted to EKA-3B standards in 1967. Rebuilt as a KA-3B at the Alameda NARF, it subsequently flew with VAW-13 (see profile 13), VAK-308 and VAQ-33 before being retired in 1989 and scrapped at Alameda as part of SARDIP.

8

KA-3B BuNo 142649/NK 104 of VAH-8, USS *Constellation* (CVA-64), 1967

VAH-8's second and third deployments to Vietnam were in *Constellation* with CVW-15 (1966) and CVW-14 (1967), respectively. The 1967 cruise was again made in squadron strength, with five aircraft assigned. With no fighter units occupying the 100 Modex numbers on this deployment (F-4B-equipped VF-92 was NK 200 and VF-96 NK 600), CVW-14 gave that series to the 'Fireballers'. This was Heavy Eight's final deployment, for the unit would be disestablished in January 1968. BuNo 142649, delivered in December 1958 as the final basic wing A3D-2, would be lost with VAQ-308 in a crash at Buckley ANGB, Colorado, on 29 October 1972.

9

KA-3B BuNo 138953/AA 615 of VAH-10 Det 59, USS *Forrestal* (CVA-59), 1967

Whidbey's 'Heavy Ten' was covering mostly Atlantic Fleet carriers by 1966, with three of its first four detachments to Vietnam being on east coast flightdecks. Its third effort in the war zone was Det 59, assigned to *Forrestal* on its first war cruise. AA 615 shows the distinctive, stylised AA tailcode markings applied to aircraft of CVW-17, which itself had only been formed a year prior. The squadron's Viking broadsword is featured as well – a trademark that would be continued for years to come. *Forrestal's* deployment was shortened by the horrific fire of 29 July 1967. Delivered to the US Navy in September 1957, BuNo 138953 would survive the conflagration and eventually end its days flying with the reserves prior to its retirement to MASDC in May 1975.

10

KA-3B BuNo 142252/NK 100 of VAH-10 Det 64, USS *Constellation* (CVA-64), December 1968

The introduction of the EKA-3B to the fleet in 1967 led to three of the new jammers being assigned by VAW-13 to most CVAs in the war zone. Increased tanking requirements meant that an additional pair of KA-3Bs was added to each air wing, and this demand was filled by assigning 'Whales' from Whidbey-based VAH units. In May 1968 *Constellation* deployed with a trio of VAW-13 EKA-3Bs and two VAH-2 KA-3Bs, with the team operating as a combined unit. In November both of Heavy Two's deployed detachments were transferred to VAH-10. NK 100 shows that Det 64 on *Constellation* quickly adopted its new parent's broadsword markings, along with blood adornment. Once again, without a VF unit employing the 100 Modex numbers, the 'Whales' were given the series for this deployment. The jet's tail stripe, however, was maroon, rather than 100 series red. BuNo 142252 entered service in February 1958 and was eventually converted into an EKA-3B in June 1969. It was lost whilst serving with VAQ-131 on 7 August 1970 when the jet suffered a control failure at high altitude over Colorado. All four crew bailed out successfully.

11

﹍H-10 Det 38,

for Vietnam from
became the only
sel to ever deploy with
he honours, operating
the 26-year-old carrier
now traditional Viking
rmal red tail stripe
1957, BuNo 138973
1975 and recycled

H-10,

outside of Alameda
y Attack unit to
nming version of the
pring of 1969, and the
th the type – to the
Saratoga, from July
ater EKA-3B
t VAQ-129. The ZR
y assigned to Heavy
ely intended for
erwise, BuNo
th fleet-going aircraft,
roadsword on the
US Navy in June 1959,
y 1978.

AW-13 Det 65,

EKA-3Bs were delivered to Alameda-based VAW-13 from mid-1967, these aircraft replacing EA-1F Skyraiders in the increasingly important EW role. Det 65 made VAW-13's second deployment to Vietnam when it embarked three EKA-3Bs in CVAN-65 in early January 1968. These jets were joined by two KA-3Bs from VAH-2 to form a combined 'Whale' unit for CVW-14. VR 27 carries the squadron's unique tailcode, while the VAH-2 aircraft on cruise wore ZA codes. As with most A-3s seen on carrier decks during the Southeast Asian conflict, BuNo 147667's tail stripe is maroon in colour.

14
EKA-3B BuNo 142651/NP 021 of VAW-13 Det 19, USS *Hancock* (CVA-19), 1968

VAW-13's Det 19 was the second EKA-3B detachment on a '27C' class carrier, with three jets assigned. Photographs strongly suggest that CVW-21 required its A-3s to carry different colours on its aircraft to distinguish the tankers when flying within large formations. NP 021 wore yellow markings, while those on NP 022 (BuNo 142662) during the same cruise

appeared to be red or orange. Confusing things even further, the det's jets wore 040 series numbers during work-ups before switching to 020 series at some point. Interestingly, the same lightning and coloured rudder motif was used by VAW-13's Det 42, which deployed to the Mediterranean in January 1970 with CVW-6 onboard *Franklin D Roosevelt*. BuNo 142651 was accepted by the US Navy in March 1959 and was placed in storage within MASDC in March 1978. Subsequently transported to the Barry M Goldwater Air Force Range in Arizona as a target, the aircraft had been destroyed by 2004.

15
EKA-3B BuNo 142657/NF 032 of VAW-13 Det 31, USS *Bon Homme Richard* (CVA-31), 1968

When 'Bonnie Dick' departed Alameda for Southeast Asia in late January 1968, it had chained down to its flightdeck the first three-aircraft detachment of EKA-3Bs to be embarked in a '27C' class carrier. Self-styled as the 'Killer Whales', the det painted its nickname on the forward fuselage of all three aircraft. Delivered to the US Navy in March 1959, BuNo 142657 was lost near Da Nang on 16 May 1970 while serving with VAQ-135, embarked in *Coral Sea*. The aircraft ran low on fuel, possibly due to bad weather, while being ferried from Cubi Point to CVA-43 in the Gulf of Tonkin. Told to divert to Da Nang, the jet disappeared off the radar and it was subsequently found to have crashed off the coast of South Vietnam. All three aircrew were listed as killed, and only one body was recovered during an extensive search of the area.

16
EKA-3B BuNo 147663/AE 715 of VAW-13 Det 66, USS *America* (CVA-66), 1968

The new 'supercarrier' *America* reported to the war zone from Norfolk in May 1968 with a mixed 'Whale' team of three VAW-13 EKA-3Bs and a pair of VAH-10 KA-3Bs from Whidbey. Markings for the 'Zapper' 'Whales' were remarkably plain other than the star spangled blue stripe on the tail. Amongst the last A-3s delivered, in November 1960, BuNo 147663 was converted into a KA-3B in September 1974 and served on with VAK-208 well into the 1980s.

17
EKA-3B BuNo 147657/NM 615 of VAQ-130 Det 34, USS *Oriskany* (CVA-34), 1969

VAW-13 was re-designated VAQ-130 in October 1968, and the 'Zappers' continued on as before by sending EKA-3B detachments to carriers headed for Vietnam. Det 34, embarked in *Oriskany*, spent most of its time working from the beach, with the result that the unit used duct tape to cross out its ship's name and crudely stencilled *DA NANG* above it (obscured here by the wingtip) on the aft ALQ-92 blister. Delivered in August 1960, BuNo 147657 was retired following the disestablishment of VAK-208 in September 1989. The jet's entire cockpit section was preserved during the SARDIP process, subsequently being acquired by Ennis Gibbs. It was transferred to the Kalamazoo Air Zoo museum in Portage, Michigan, in June 2013, where it will be restored and eventually put on display.

18
EKA-3B BuNo 142634/NE 611 of VAQ-130 Det 4, USS *Ranger* (CVA-61), 1972-73

In early 1973 EKA-3Bs started losing their distinctive ALQ-92 side blisters as the system was removed from the aircraft. The surgery led to oblong sheet metal 'scars' on the aircraft, as seen here. Retention of the ALT-27 jammer system in the belly meant they were still EKA-3Bs, although many would eventually lose this as well and be converted back to full KA-3B status for work with the reserves in the mid-1970s. Delivered in May 1958, this aircraft would be lost in a failed catapult shot from *Ranger* in the Gulf of Tonkin on 21 January 1973 which resulted in the loss of all three crew. NE 611 shows VAQ-130's final EKA-3B markings, with twin black tail stripes.

19
EKA-3B BuNo 142659/NP 616 of VAQ-129 Det 19, USS *Hancock* (CVA-19), 1970-71

VAH-10 was re-designated VAQ-129 on 1 September 1970, with two KA-3B detachments (embarked in *Shangri-La* and *Independence*) making the change while underway. In October VAQ-129 deployed its only 'Whale' detachment under the new designation, sending three EKA-3Bs to *Hancock* as part of CVW-21. The squadron retained Heavy Ten's 'Vikings' nickname and broadsword markings. In keeping with CVW-21 policy, each aircraft in Det 19 was marked slightly differently in order to help receiving pilots tell the tankers apart in flight. NP 614 (BuNo 144628) had a red tick marking, NP 615 (BuNo 142650) had its marking in white and NP 616 (depicted here) used medium blue. All three jets had a red tail stripe adorned with white stars. By the time the detachment returned home from the Far East in June 1971 the squadron was operating as the US Navy's EA-6B Prowler training outfit. BuNo 142659, which had been delivered in April 1959, was destroyed at Alameda on 10 July 1977 when it crashed into San Francisco Bay during an aborted takeoff. The aircraft was serving with VAQ-308 at the time.

20
KA-3B BuNo 138941/NH 612 of VAQ-131, USS *Kitty Hawk* (CVA-63), 1968-69

VAH-4 was re-designated VAQ-131 on 1 November 1968 and duly moved to Alameda to join the new EKA-3B community. With its first deployment only a month away, the squadron did not waste time on a new logo or nickname. It simply retained a slightly modified version of Heavy Four's insignia, as well as adopting its 'Holly Green' radio call-sign as its nickname. The unit was assigned to *Kitty Hawk* and CVW-11 for an almost nine-month cruise to the war zone, flying three EKA-3Bs and a pair of KA-3Bs from CVA-63. Initially numbered with single digits, these aircraft were quickly adorned with the new standard 610 series modex numbers directed for VAQ aircraft. The resulting renumbering led to several of the squadron's 'Whales' not wearing matching numbers and stripes – a cosmetic issue that took several months to fix by cycling aircraft through the Japanese contractor NIPPI. In September 1970 VAQ-131 deployed to the Mediterranean in *John F Kennedy*, returning in February 1971 to move to Whidbey Island for EA-6B transition. Once here the unit finally adopted a new nickname ('Lancers') and insignia. Accepted for service by the US Navy in June 1957, BuNo 138941 made both deployments with VAQ-131 and was then promptly retired upon the unit's return to Alameda in January 1971. The aircraft was duly salvaged at NARF Norfolk.

21
EKA-3B BuNo 142404/NG 616 of VAQ-132, USS *America* (CVA-66), 1970

VAH-2 was re-designated VAQ-132 on 1 November 1968 to provide a five-aircraft squadron to big-deck carriers. Unlike sister-squadron VAQ-131, however, the unit quickly adopted a new nickname ('Scorpions') and logo to go with its new identity. The squadron made two deployments with a mix of EKA-3Bs and KA-3Bs as a member of CVW-9 in *Enterprise* and then *America*. The 'Scorps' moved to Whidbey in early 1971 and subsequently became the first fleet EA-6B squadron. Fully marked aircraft featured this striking red paint scheme, with the tail BuNo in this case being applied in dark grey. Delivered in March 1958, BuNo 142404 was sent to MASDC in

December 1973 and eventually disposed of as a target on the Barry M Goldwater Air Force Range in Arizona in 2004.

22
KA-3B BuNo 138966/NH 611 of VAQ-133, USS *Kitty Hawk* (CVA-63), 1970-71

VAQ-133 was established on 4 March 1969, with its core personnel coming from VAQ-130 Det 64. It was assigned five aircraft (three EKA-3Bs and two KA-3Bs) and made two deployments to Vietnam, before heading north for EA-6B transition. Although the unit's 'flying cocktail fork' insignia (seen here beneath the cockpit of the aircraft) was approved in 1970, squadron documents refer to the unit as the 'Golden Zappers' prior to adoption of the later, and more familiar, 'Wizard' nickname. The distinctive tail markings seen on this aircraft were a feature of VAQ-133's second deployment, and in photographs from the period they range in colour from a deep, rich maroon (the squadron's primary shade) to black. BuNo 138966 was accepted by the US Navy in July 1957, and the aircraft served until February 1974, when it was salvaged at NARF Alameda.

23
EKA-3B BuNo 142649/NE 615 of VAQ-134, USS *Ranger* (CVA-61), 1970-71

The sixth, and last, new VAQ unit established at Alameda in the late 1960s was VAQ-134, which had the former VAQ-130 Det 61 at the heart of its formation. The first squadron CO chose a Garuda – a mythical Indonesian creature – as the unit nickname and designed a logo to go with the title. NE 615, from the unit's second cruise, boasts full markings, including a thin maroon stripe on the tail as well as a yellow 'bird' flash. VAQ-134 made two 'Whale' deployments before transferring to Whidbey for EA-6B transition. Delivered in December 1958, BuNo 142649 was destroyed in a crash at Buckley ANGB, Colorado, on 29 October 1972 while serving with VAQ-308.

24
EKA-3B BuNo 142404/NL 612 of VAQ-135 Det 3, USS *Coral Sea* (CVA-43), 1971-72

VAQ-135 was established on 17 May 1969 from VAQ-130 Det 43, becoming the fifth unit formed at Alameda to fly EKA-3Bs. The new squadron went right back to *Coral Sea* with four aircraft – three EKA-3Bs and a single KA-3B. This 1969-70 cruise proved to be the only one it made as a full squadron, VAQ-135 then becoming a detachment provider from late 1970. Its jets duly filled the flightdeck slots being opened up by the exodus of other VAQs to Whidbey for Prowler conversion. This profile depicts an aircraft from Det 3 serving with CVW-15 onboard CVA-43 in 1971-72, BuNo 142404 (also see in profile 21) featuring VAQ-135's modest early unit markings that consisted of nothing more than maroon stripes on the tail and the squadron logo on the forward ALQ-92 blister. At this time the unit was better known by its 'Homebrew' radio call-sign – the more familiar 'Black Raven' title would come later.

25
EKA-3B BuNo 142656/NP 614 of VAQ-135 Det 5, USS *Hancock* (CVA-19), 1973

VAQ-135 Det 2, which deployed to the Mediterranean in *Forrestal*, is given credit in squadron records for coining the 'Black Raven' nickname that was soon adopted by the entire unit. The det was also the first to mark the tails of its jets with the large, hook-nosed raven design seen here. This emblem, combined with the sky blue stripes on the forward fuselage and fin tip, became one of the more attractive schemes applied to a Skywarrior. Only three dets (in

Forrestal, Coral Sea and *Hancock*) had the chance to take these markings to sea before the unit moved to Whidbey Island, leaving VAQ-130 as the last EKA-3B operator at Alameda. When not assigned to a specific detachment at home, VAQ-135's aircraft appeared with VAQW-13's TR tailcode. NP 614 is from Det 3, the squadron's last A-3 deployment, which embarked in *Hancock* in May 1973. The ALQ-92 blisters have been removed, although the belly-mounted ALT-27 package remains. The aircraft has a red tail cone in accordance with CVW-21 tanker marking policy. Presumably the other two aircraft on the detachment were painted differently, with their tail cones possibly in blue and white. BuNo 142656 served with the US Navy from March 1959 through to May 1975, when it was retired to MASDC.

26
KA-3B BuNo 138923/ND 630 of VAQ-308, NAS Cubi Point, the Philippines, 1971
Probably the least documented A-3 users in Vietnam were the two reserve KA-3B outfits formed at Alameda in 1970. Both squadrons, VAQ-208 and VAQ-308, sent jets to WestPac during the war's last two-and-half years as navigation ('pathfinding') leads for smaller aircraft on long-distance transits, as well as providing tanker coverage out of Cubi Point and 'Fast COD' logistics support for carriers on *Yankee Station*. Although designated as VAQ units, both outfits flew only KA-3Bs. Indeed, they never received the EKA, the reserve EW mission eventually being covered by new EA-6A squadrons VAQ-209 and VAQ-309. Both 'Whale' units would be re-designated as tanker (VAK) squadrons on 1 October 1979 and continue flying A-3s until disestablished in September 1989. ND 630 is depicted here in the markings it wore during a visit to WestPac in 1971. CVWR-30's attractively stylised 'November Delta' tailcode stands out, as does the use of a large zero on the tail to represent the last digit of the aircraft's side number. Other aircraft in the squadron carried large roman numerals (I, II, III or IV) in the same location. Delivered in February 1957, BuNo 138923 was retired in June 1973 and scrapped shortly thereafter.

27
RA-3B BuNo 144826/SS 904 of VAP-61, Da Nang, South Vietnam, 1965
Aircraft of Heavy Photographic Squadron 61 entered the Vietnam War with very simple markings, as represented here by SS 904. The unit's hazardous missions over North Vietnam soon led to its RA-3Bs being hastily camouflaged. Accepted by the US Navy in June 1959, BuNo 144826 was lost on 8 August 1969 following a dual engine flame-out (caused by fuel flow problems) at high altitude while on a logistics flight from Da Nang. All four crew bailed out and were recovered.

28
RA-3B BuNo 144847, VAP-61, NAS Cubi Point, the Philippines, 1966
Early in the war VAP-61 realised that the standard grey and white US Navy camouflage scheme was too conspicuous for its specialised mission, which frequently entailed flight at low altitudes over North Vietnam at night. According to squadron lore a crew at Cubi Point painted an RA-3B dull black with spray cans and reported it as being far better suited to their nocturnal operations. Other aircraft were duly repainted through more deliberate means, possibly at contractor NIPPI in Japan. Details like side numbers and tailcodes were not carried, and not all aircraft had the squadron designation applied. The black scheme was soon replaced by officially approved mottled camouflage applied to aircraft at NARF Alameda. Unfortunately, the exact number of aircraft re-sprayed in either camouflage scheme remains unknown. In spite of the special paint, BuNo 144847 (which was delivered in April 1960) was hit by ground fire over North Vietnam during a night reconnaissance mission on 1 January 1968. Crashing into the sea 30 miles off Dong Hoi, no trace of the aircraft, or its three-man crew, was ever found.

29
RA-3B BuNo 144831 of VAP-61, Da Nang, South Vietnam, 1969
By roughly mid-1968 the A-3 depot at Alameda had designed a multi-toned camouflage scheme for large US Navy aircraft involved in low altitude night work over Vietnam, which included VAP-61 RA-3Bs and VAH-21 AP-2Hs. It appears that the scheme was not well received by VAP-61 crews, who felt overall black was a better treatment. Nevertheless, a number of RA-3Bs flew combat missions in this scheme until VAP-61 was removed from Vietnam in 1970. Several such camouflaged RA-3Bs were transferred to VQ-1 when VAP-61 was disestablished in July 1971. Delivered in September 1959, BuNo 144831 was retired in June 1976 and salvaged by NARF Alameda.

30
EA-3B BuNo 146459/PR 4 of VQ-1, Da Nang, South Vietnam, 1966
VQ-1's markings remained remarkably consistent throughout the Vietnam War. They were also predictably simple, befitting the unit's desire to remain unnoticed as it went about its work. Other than the jet's 'Peter Rabbit' tailcode and single digit side number, there were no distinctive markings applied to VQ-1's aircraft until after the war had ended. PR 4 was BuNo 146459, the 24th, and last, production A3D-2Q built (and delivered in July 1960), half of which had cambered leading edge wings. It would be one of the last 'Whales' on active duty, finally being retired to the Aircraft Maintenance And Regeneration Center at Davis-Monthan AFB in September 1991.

INDEX